KALONGA GAWA UNDI X

KALONGA GAWA UNDI X
A BIOGRAPHY OF AN AFRICAN CHIEF AND NATIONALIST

WALIMA T. KALUSA

IN COLLABORATION WITH THE LATE MAPOPA MTONGA

The Lembani Trust
LUSAKA

http://sites.google.com/site/lembanitrust/

Published in 2010 by the Lembani Trust
Lusaka, Zambia

ISBN 978-9982-9972-5-6

Cover and book design by Lawrence Dritsas

Lembani Trust books are distributed worldwide by the African Books Collective
www.africanbookscollective.com

Contents

Illustrations

*All photographs are reproduced with the kind permission of
the National Archives of Zambia*

Foreword

In 2009 the Lembani Trust, the publication wing of the Network for Historical Research in Zambia, published *One Zambia, Many Histories: Towards a History of Post Colonial Zambia*. The choice of the title is quite informative in that it not only borrows from Zambia's motto of "One Zambia One Nation", but brings to mind the fact that the country has many histories. Some of these histories are yet to be written and published. Indeed, as Robert Ross wrote in its Foreword, 'Zambia may have remained one nation, but that nation's history is much more complicated than the rulers under UNIP would have had us believe – and also more complicated than the post-UNIP rulers would agree, so that a story of continued struggle against a monolithic state would also not apply.'

Arguably, *Kalonga Gawa Undi X: A Biography of an African Chief and Nationalist*, fits into the observation by Ross in the sense that this study highlights the different approaches that traditional authorities took *vis-à-vis* the struggle for independence in Zambia. This book takes a different approach and demonstrates that thus far, and with respect to the role that Kalonga Gawa Undi X played, the Chewa Chief was not a just a willing pawn in the struggle for independence. On the contrary, he was in his own right a nationalist who fought for the independence of Zambia – for reasons that did not always mesh with those of political nationalist elites who spearheaded the anti-colonial struggle.

The book is a timely reminder that historians of Zambia need to revisit the long-settled interpretations of Zambian colonial history with a view to writing the many histories that characterized the various contours of the country's past. It should be noted that African chiefs have attracted scholarly attention in the studies of colonialism and the role that they played. What is contested in this study is the generalization that traditional authorities were little more than pawns in the hands the nationalist elites during the struggle for freedom from imperial hegemony.

Dr Kalusa's conclusion to this work gives a carefully-argued analysis to the theme of the book. It is an analysis that historians will find worth reading and unlikely to refute easily.

Professor Bizeck Jube Phiri (PhD)

Chronology

1931 On 1 January Obister Chivunga Phiri is born at Chambobo village on the Zambia-Mozambique border.

1949 His cousin, Chisaka, is killed in a motorcycle accident at Chassa, Eastern province. Obister is recalled by the Chewa royal family from his teacher training course at Chalimbana in Lusaka

1950 Obister Chivunga Phiri begins working as a clerk under his uncle, Gawa Undi IX Chimphungu

1952 Gawa Undi IX Chimpungu dies. Obister Chivunga Phiri becomes Chief Designate and presides over the selection and enthronement of Kambauwa as Chief Kawaza. As Chief Designate,he writes letters to the District Commissioner in Chipata and to Chewa chiefs in Malawi to defend his claim to the Undiship.

1953 On 3 March Obister Chivunga Phiri is enthroned as Gawa Undi X. In the same year, the Federation of Rhodesia and Nyasaland is created by European settlers against strong African opposition

1954 Gawa Undi X mediates the selection and enthronement of Uliya as Chief Mbango'mbe

1955 The Paramount Chief attends the Livingstone centenary celebrations in Livingstone in colonial Zambia.

1956 Gawa Undi X goes to England to study local administration at Torquay, South Devon

1957 Paramount Chief Undi X visits Rome and the Vatican, returns to Katete, and joins the African nationalist movement

1958 The Paramount Chief attends Federal constitutional talks in England.

1960 Gawa Undi X attends Lancaster House independence talks, boycotts the Moncton Commission,, and welcomes the Queen mother in Salisbury (Harare)

1963 The Federation of Rhodesia and Nyasaland is dismantled

1964 On 24 October Northern Rhodesia becomes the independent state of Zambia

1965 On 9 December The Paramount Chief condemns Ian Smith's Unilateral Declaration of Independence (UDI) in colonial Zimbabwe

1966 Gawa Undi X strongly opposes the Local Authority and Court Bills. He also receives from President Kenneth Kaunda the insignia of Officer of Distinguished Service (O.D.S.)

1967 The Chewa ruler serves as Secretary on the Chipata District Council

1968 Gawa Undi X becomes Chairman of the House of Chiefs

1971 In August Simon Mwansa Kapwepwe breaks away from UNIP to form the United Progressive Party (UPP). On 12 November Gawa Undi X delivers a biting speech in the House of Chiefs opposing the formation of the United Progressive Party (UPP). He is later appointed as a member of the constitutional review commission tasked to examine the introduction of one-party state in Zambia

1972 In August President Kaunda bans the UPP. In December Zambia becomes a one-party state through the Choma Declaration

1975 Gawa Undi X makes a pilgrimage to Rome and the Vatican to meet the Pope. He also visits the the Holy Land, and Lourdes, France, to see where the Virgin Mary is said to have spoken to Bernadette

1981 The Chewa Paramount Chief steps down as Chairman of House of Chiefs

1984 The chief successfully calls for the reviving of the Kulamba ceremony of the Chewa people

1985 In August the first Kulamba ceremony is held at Mkaika, Katete, after many decades of not being celebrated

1995 On 3 September Gawa Undi X installs Henry Kalinga Phiri as Senior Chief Mwase X

2002 On 24 October President Levy Mwanawasa confers the Presidential Insignia of Honour on Gawa Undi X

2003 On 3 March Golden Jubilee celebrations take place at Mkaika to mark the 50th year of the Chief's leadership. In August Gawa Undi X falls sick and is admitted to St. Francis Hospital in Katete and later to the University Teaching Hospital in Lusaka

2004 President Patrick Levy Mwanawasa attends the Kulamba ceremony for the first time. On 21 November Gawa Undi X dies. Soon after, on 2 December his grandnephew, Frederic Daka, succeeds the late chief. December 3rd 2004, Gawa Undi X is buried at Dole in Katete district

Preface

This book attempts to reconstruct the life experiences of Kalonga Gawa Undi X *né* Obister Chivunga Phiri, the Paramount Chief of the Chewa-speaking people in Zambia's Eastern province, whose reign began in 1953 and ended with his death in 2004. The study distances itself from the all-too-familiar academic scholarship that projects traditional authorities in colonial and post-colonial settings as mere cogs in the wheels of state power. To the contrary, it shows that even though the ideologies and praxis of the Chewa potentate were profoundly shaped by social, economic and political dynamics connected with colonial and post-colonial power, he acted upon these very dynamics to forge his own destiny and that of his people and country. This insulates Kalonga Gawa Undi X from academic discourse that caricatures chiefs in Africa as rulers who have historically been willing pawns of centralised power, and therefore acquiesced in their own domination.

This study traces its birth to the late President Levy Patrick Mwanawasa's directive to the Office of the Vice-President in 2004 to assemble a team of researchers to write a biography of Kalonga Gawa Undi X. This directive issued from his recognition of the significant role the Chewa traditional leader played in the struggle for Zambia's independence between 1957 and 1964. It is in light of this recognition that this book was conceived and nurtured by Professor Mapopa Mtonga and myself. Sadly, President Mwanawasa and Professor Mtonga, who initially spearheaded the research out of which this book has grown, passed away in 2008 before its publication. The study is posthumously dedicated to them. It must also be noted that before moving to the House of Chiefs, the Gawa Undi X Book Project was coordinated by Hon. Rose Banda, the former Deputy Minister in the Office of the Vice-President.

Many individuals have made the publication of this study possible. Among those who deserve a special pat on the back are Dr Joshua Kanganja, the Secretary to the Cabinet; Mr Collaird Chilala Chibbonta, the Clerk at the House of Chiefs; and Dr Patrick Francis Manda, the Research Officer at House of Chiefs. In more ways than may be enumerated here, they individually and collectively encouraged me to complete the Gawa

Undi Book Project after the demise of Professor Mapopa Mtonga. Similar heart-felt thanks extend to Dr Francis Musonda of the University of Zambia, who patiently read and commented on some of the chapters in this volume. Mr Galeta Chikuta Mbewe, Mr Lyson Chigaga Phiri, and Mr. Fasten Phiri equally deserve a pat on the back. Without their deep knowledge of Chewa customs, history and politics, it would have been practically impossible to complete this book. Also I wish to express my profound gratitude to Dr Lawrence Dritsas for typesetting this book.

Finally, I wish to express my gratitude to Dr Webby S. Kalikiti, Dr Euston Kasongo Chiputa and Mr. Clarence Chongo of the History Department at the University of Zambia. Each of them generously shared their research notes with me.

Walima T. Kalusa
Lusaka, 2008

List of Abbreviations

ANC	African National Congress
DC	District Commissioner
EP	Eastern Province
FRELIMO	Frente de Libertação de Moçambique
MMD	Movement for Multi-party Democracy
MNR	Mozambican National Resistance
NAZ	National Archives of Zambia
PC	Provincial Commissioner
UDI	Unilateral Declaration of Independence
UNIP	United National Independence Party
UPP	United Progressive Party
ODS	Officer of Distinguished Service
RENAMO	Resistência Nacional Moçambicana
SEC	Secretariat
UK	United Kingdom
ZANC	Zambia African National Congress
ZMM-GT	Zambia-Malawi-Mozambique Growth Triangle

1

Introduction

Chiefs in African Historiography

In his seminal study, *Citizen and Subject*, Mahmood Mamdani, one of Africa's leading contemporary analysts, categorically asserts that colonialism transformed African traditional authorities into agents of imperial domination. Rather than weakening or democratising the chiefly office, colonial rule, Mamdani insists, reinforced chiefly authority, prestige and power. As a corollary, holders of the chiefly office came to constitute the vanguard of what he describes as "decentralised despotism". The Ugandan scholar concludes that such despotism was as much the cornerstone of colonial power as it has both outlived Western imperial hegemony and buttressed dictatorial regimes in post-colonial Africa.[1]

Though presented with rare elegance and sophistication, Mamdani's polemic is neither new nor peculiar to British Africa on which his study mostly focuses. Long before he published it in 1996, many other academics working on the societies far removed in time and space similarly maintained that across the continent, European colonisers reinvented traditional authority and customary law to serve their own interests and those of the metropole, as opposed to the interests of the subjects of the Western empire.[2] In such analyses, traditional rulers emerged as no more than instruments of imperial control, who acquiesced in European domination and in the subjugation of their own subjects.

Scholarship that dismisses indigenous authorities on the periphery of the European Empire from the 19th century onwards as mere appendages

---

[1] Mahmood Mamdani, *Citizen and Subject: Contemporary Africa and the Legacy of Late Colonialism* (Princeton, New Jersey: Princeton University Press, 1996).

[2] See, for example, Eric Hobsbawm and Terence Ranger (ed.), *The Invention of Tradition* (Cambridge: Cambridge University Press, 1983); Martin Chanock, *Law, Custom and Social Order: The Colonial Experience in Malawi and Zambia* (Cambridge: Cambridge University Press, 1985). See also Sara Berry, "Unsettled Accounts: Debt Stool, Chieftaincy Disputes and the Question of Asante Constitutionalism," *Journal of African Studies* 39 (1998), p. 39-42.

of centralised state power cannot escape criticism. This is because, as some analysts have correctly observed in recent decades, traditional rulers under imperial rule neither constituted a monolithic entity nor shared homogenous interests. Chiefs held fundamentally conflicting attitudes, ideologies and approaches towards colonial states and the people over whom they reigned.[3] While some traditional authorities certainly welcomed colonial rule, seeing it as a source of additional power, others sometimes embraced it only to contest against it later, often with dire political and economic consequences.[4] Local authorities' responses to colonial intrusion, therefore, varied in time and space, a point that Ghanaian historian Adu Boahen makes most poignantly in his exploration of African perspectives on colonialism in various parts of the continent. As Boahen emphatically argues, their attitudes to imperial hegemony were far from uniform. This is because chiefs' apprehensions of colonialism were driven by conflicting motives, by individual or collective needs, and by the particular situations in which the rulers found themselves.[5]

Boahen's perspectives are aptly illustrated by the life history of Kalonga Gawa Undi X *né* Obister Chivunga Phiri, the subject of this biography. Paramount Chief of the Chewa in Zambia's Eastern province from 1953 to 2004, Kalonga Gawa Undi X reacted to centralised power both in the colonial and post colonial periods in accordance with prevailing situations and his own needs. To be sure, the Paramount Chief hardly questioned British colonial rule in the first four years of his reign. During this time, he, as chapter two in this volume shows, distanced himself from the rapidly gathering storm of African nationalism by maintaining an anti-nationalist posture. It is also equally true that during his early leadership, the Chewa Chief embraced colonially-engineered institutions, including the Native Authorities, the Eastern Provincial Council of Chiefs, and, after 1962, the House of Chiefs. But his perception of these institutions diametrically differed with that of the architects of the British colonialism, who crafted these very institutions. For if the coloniser regarded Native Authorities and other related organs as instruments of political hegemony, the potentate himself saw them as a means by which he could ameliorate his, and his

---

[3] Samuel N. Chipungu, "African Leadership under Indirect Rule in Colonial Zambia," in Samuel N. Chipungu (ed.), *Guardians in their Time: Experiences of Zambians under Colonial Rule* (London: Macmillan, 1992), pp. 50-74.

[4] Adu Boahen, *African Perspectives on Colonialism* (Baltimore: Johns Hopkins University Press, 1978); T.O. Ranger, *Revolt in Southern Rhodesia, 1896-7* (London: Heinemann, 1967). See also his "The Mwana Lesa Movement of 1925," in T. O. Ranger and J. Weller (eds.), *Themes in the Christian History of Central Africa* (Berkeley and Los Angeles: University of California Press, 1975), pp. 45-75.

[5] Boahen, *African Perspectives*.

subjects' socio-economic welfare and, after he joined the anti-colonial protest in 1957, to contest colonial power.

To Kalonga Gawa Undi X, therefore, the institutions associated with European colonialism were not instruments of imperial control. Nor was missionary education with its underlying belief system. Thus, even though the sovereign embraced mission education and Christianity early in his life, he contested the hegemonic agenda that underscored modern education and Christianity on the imperial frontier. In so doing, he subverted the hegemonic intentions of European authorities and missionaries, whose primary aim was to deploy education with its religious ideology to politically subdue African societies, to annihilate their culture, and to supplant their local belief systems with Euro-Christian bourgeois values and beliefs.

Contrary to the expectations of the European agents of the British Empire, Kalonga Gawa Undi X invested his own meanings and uses into Western education, Christianity and other colonial institutions. He consequently transformed them from being an instrument of colonial control into a vehicle for bolstering the social and economic welfare of his subjects without either undermining his own authority, or forsaking his cultural heritage. Kalonga Gawa Undi X would most vividly mark his deep devotion to African culture by reviving the Kulamba ceremony two decades before his death in 2004. This was notwithstanding that this cultural form was earlier condemned by missionaries as a citadel of "paganism," had been defunct for fifty years, and, most importantly, Gawa Undi X himself was a devout Christian.[6]

As noted earlier, the Chewa Paramount Chief initially hoped to foster the socio-economic welfare of his people within the realm of colonialism. But nowhere in extra-European settings was imperial rule designed to benefit its subjects. This fact dawned on Kalonga Gawa Undi X by the late 1950s. Unsurprisingly, he henceforth turned into a bitter critic of British political supremacy in Africa. This study shows that this shift in the political perspective of the traditional ruler was the consequence of both internal and external dynamics. Of crucial importance among the external forces was the formal and informal education the Chewa potentate received when he attended a course in local administration in England from 1956 to 1957. There, as later demonstrated, he was exposed to advanced political ideas articulated by classmates from other parts of the British Empire, who left no stone unturned in condemning colonial subjugation in Africa. These

---

[6] See chapter 6.

ideas seem to have brought into sharp relief in the mind of Kalonga Gawa Undi X the draconian and undemocratic ways under which Britain governed Africans in colonial Zambia.

By the time the Paramount Chief returned to colonial Zambia from Europe in 1957, he seems to have already turned into a disciple of the gospel of African nationalism, intent on eradicating British domination. His commitment to annihilating colonial misrule was fuelled by such internal dynamics as the growing clamouring among European white settlers in the colony for a dominion status in the 1950s and 1960s, and by their deep abhorrence towards African demands for political freedom. To nip in the bud the settlers' penchant for self-government, Kalonga Gawa Undi X joined the African National Congress (ANC) in 1957. A year later, he switched his allegiance to the Zambia African National Congress (ZANC), the forerunner of the United National Independence Party (UNIP) that seemed to be more militant in its quest for independence from Britain than the ANC.

The suzerain's strategies in the struggle against foreign domination widely diverged from those pursued by urban-based nationalist elite. Unlike the elite who indiscriminately sought to eradicate all colonial institutions, including Native Authorities and the Council of Chiefs, Kalonga Gawa Undi X pragmatically saw them as a weapon he could wield to challenge alien rule, and, as earlier noted, to promote African socio-economic welfare and the authority of the chiefly office. Ironically, it was through these very institutions that European authorities across British Africa hoped to roll back the suffocating whirlwind of African nationalism.

The ambiguity that marked the Paramount Chief's attitude to colonialism together with its institutions from the late 1950s onwards did not die with the collapse of British political ascendancy, or with the emergence of independent Zambia in 1964. For, although the Chewa overlord supported successive post-colonial regimes in Zambia well up to his death in 2004, he also sought to carve for himself and, of course, for other traditional authorities, some measure of political autonomy from the regimes. It is in this vein that one may appreciate why after independence, Kalonga Gawa Undi X frequently raised his voice against legislation that he perceived as inimical to the chiefly office. For example, he vehemently opposed the Local Government and Local Courts Acts passed by President Kenneth Kaunda's UNIP leaders in the mid-1960s in their quest to boost centralised control at the expense of the authority, power and prestige of chiefs. To the Paramount

Chief, such legislation was little more than a ploy by the UNIP-dominated regime to monopolise power. In spite of the ill-feeling that the legislation spawned between Kalonga Gawa Undi X and the Zambian state, however, the former continued to be supportive of the Kaunda regime, and its successors. This support manifested itself in his unfailing endeavour to uplift the welfare of his people through policies and institutions designed by the successive regimes.

Unsurprisingly, the Paramount Chief played a no minor role in enforcing the domestic and foreign policies in Zambia's post-colonial era even as he contested the regimes' propensity to monopolise power at the expense of traditional rulers. This became particularly obvious from the 1970s onward, when he began to have doubts about the ability of the post-colonial regime in Zambia to contain rising poverty and corruption in Zambia. In maintaining an ambiguous stance toward successive post-colonial states, the potentate carved for himself sufficient political space within which he could both buttress state policies that he perceived as desirable and yet oppose those that he deemed detrimental to traditional authorities, to his people, and to the country as a whole.

In view of the foregoing observations, the life history of Kalonga Gawa Undi X serves as a corrective to academic works that all too often dismiss indigenous rulers in imperial and post-colonial settings as mere collaborators of state power. His unusual ability to foster the interests of his subjects through institutions forged by colonial and post-colonial states, while simultaneously battling the excesses of the architects of those very institutions, means that it would be wrong to write him off as a simple creation of centralised power. This insulates him from popular academic discourse that caricatures traditional ruling elites in Africa as passive stooges who have historically been accomplices in their own domination, and in the subjugation of their own people.

A Brief History of the Chewa Kingdom

Long before the whites arrived, Undi was the paramount chief of the Maravi peoples. The Chewa, Nsenga, Chipeta, Kasungu, Nyanja and all other people of the Maravi ancestry, were all below Undi's chieftainship. Many chiefs of all areas were appointed by Undi...[7]

---

[7] NAZ EP4/7/13/, Chewa students at the Jeans Teachers Training Centre, Chalimbana, Lusaka, 14 January 1953.

The Chewa, over whom Kalonga Gawa Undi X came to preside from 1953 to his death in 2004, are one of the Bantu social formations who trace their remote origins to the Luba kingdom in the present-day Democratic Republic of Congo. Their more recent origins are, however, associated with the Maravi kingdom believed to have been founded by Kalonga in modern Malawi sometime before the 15th century.[8] Why, when and how the Chewa migrated from the Luba kingdom is a matter for conjecture. A leading authority on Chewa history suggests that they may have left the Luba kingdom before 1450 and acquired the name "Maravi" after settling near Lake Malawi.[9] Oral accounts memorialise Mazizi as the founder of the Maravi kingdom. Most likely, it was Mazizi who first assumed the title "Kalonga," (loosely, "Great Chief" or "King") perhaps after he vanquished or assimilated the autochthones that he and his followers encountered in Malawi.[10] The Maravi had by the 15th century transformed the loose political system they found among the proto-Malawi people into a relatively well organised but decentralised kingdom. At its peak in that century, the kingdom seems to have stretched from as far as the southern end of Lake Malawi to central and northern Mozambique.

The circumstances under which the people who over time acquired the appellation "Chewa" separated from the Kalonga kingdom are obscure. Historians, however, agree that by the time the Chewa migrated perhaps before 1600, the Kalonga kingdom might have begun to disintegrate.[11] Its political woes may have been precipitated by the departure of Chisakamzondi Msenya Undi, whom Chewa court historians believe to have engineered the split. According to royal court discourse, Undi not only took with him Nyangu or Queen Mother, but the entire royal lineage (Mbumba).[12] Succession to the Kalongaship in Malawi henceforth came to rest in the hands of Undi's royal lineage. Subsequently, Chisakamzondi

---

[8] For a fuller and sophisticated analysis of the origins, establishment and collapse of the Chewa kingdom, see Henry Wells Langworthy III, A History of Undi's Kingdom to 1890: Aspects of Chewa History in East and Central Africa," PhD dissertation: Boston University, 1969. See also M.G. Marwick, "History and Tradition in East Central Africa through the eyes of the Northern Rhodesia Chewa," *Journal of African History* 4, 3 (1963), pp. 375-390. The discussion on the rise and fall of the Chewa kingdom draws largely on these studies and oral sources.

[9] Langworthy III, "History," p. 109.

[10] According to Chewa court traditions, Mazizi was succeeded by Kalonga Chinkhole, who in turn was followed by Chidzodzi and Mazura. Kalonga Mazura was, according to these traditions succeeded by Chikasamzondi Gawa Undi. It is impossible to verify the accuracy of this genealogy due to the absence of supporting documented evidence.

[11] Langworthy III, "History".

[12] Interview with Lyson Chigaga Phiri, Headman/Senior Advisor to Kalonga Gawa Undi, Mwanza-ulungu village, Katete, 06 August 2008; Joseph Galeta Chikuta Mbewe, Senior Advisor to Gawa Undi, Mkaika palace, 06 August 2008.

Undi and his successors played a no minor role in the political affairs of the waning Kalonga kingdom in Malawi, choosing its heirs and similarly appropriating the title of Kalonga.

It is not certain why Chisakamzondi Undi broke away from the Kalonga-Maravi kingdom. Oral traditions suggest that his migration was prompted by conflicts between the incumbent Kalonga and Undi himself, not the least of which were political and succession wrangles. It is probable, too, that the two leaders differed over the control of the important rain-making shrine at Msinja. But Chisakamzondi Undi, whom Chewa oral traditions memorialise as an ambitious man, could have also left on his volition to found his own polity or to better his economic prospects elsewhere. This suggestion is supported by the fact that he eventually settled at Mano in the area between the Kapoche River in Zambia and the Liuye River in Mozambique's Tete province close to the Portuguese in the Zambezi valley. The decision to occupy this area could have been influenced by the desire to trade with the Portuguese, who, having established outposts at Sofala, Sena and Tete in the valley in the first half of 16th century, were eager to do business with local rulers.[13]

Whatever the case, by the inception of that century, the Chewa under Kalonga Gawa Undi had certainly successfully carved for themselves a vast empire. At the zenith of the empire, its boundaries stretched roughly from modern Zambia's Eastern province through central Malawi to the northern part of the Tete province of Mozambique. It was in the latter country that the founder of the empire established the kingdom's headquarters at Mano in Tete province. It is here, too, that Chisakamzondi most likely took the title of Gawa, or "divider" to mark the fact that he dispensed land and political offices to his subordinates, whom he sent to rule the outlaying areas of his expanding kingdom.

Behind the creation of this vast empire were internal and external dynamics. Internally, the Chewa enormously benefitted from the area which they occupied. For it was endowed with natural resources ranging from good soils, ivory, gold, and rivers rich in fish and other aquatic resources like reeds. The availability of these resources was crucial to the development of local industries, including basket-making, mining, fishing and agriculture. Similarly, the absence of tsetse flies in the expanding empire permitted animal husbandry.[14]

---

[13] Langworthy III, "History".
[14] Ibid, "History," p. 307.

7

But Kalonga Gawa Undi's Chewa Empire may have owed its birth and growth more to the political dexterity of its creators. Under successive Undis, political power came to be concentrated in the Phiri clan.[15] Furthermore, they established tributary kings or chiefs by allocating conquered territories to members of the Phiri clan who distinguished themselves in either battle or in diplomacy. To integrate into the polity the autochthones they encountered where they settled, the ruling elites allowed the Banda clan, whose members were most likely long-established in the area before the arrival of the invaders, to retain their ritual authority. Such authority was regarded as critical to the fertility of the land and of its people.[16]

Chewa oral traditions indicate that Kalong Gawa Undi dispensed both land and political titles to his subordinates. Among the beneficiaries included Chulu and Mwase Kasungu in Malawi and Mwase Lundazi in Zambia. It is likely, too, that the first ruler of the chiefdom of Mkanda, whose territory spanned the modern Zambia-Malawi border, also received his political office from Gawa Undi, even though a descendant of his would vehemently dispute this point in the 1950s.[17] Other chiefs to whom Kalonga Gawa Undi awarded political titles and territories in Zambia were Kangulu, Chilekwele and Chimwala.[18] He also recognised such non-Chewa speaking chiefs like Kalindawalo of the Nsenga in Zambia's Petauke district. Lastly, Undi granted political titles to other non-Chewa chiefs, including those among the Senga and Tumbuka in Chama district and the Bisa along the Mchinga Escarpment.[19]

Politically, the Phiri clan and the royal family wielded political influence and power over tributary kings and chiefs alike. For example, the selection and the enthronement of subordinate rulers were the royal family's prerogative. In contrast, tributary chiefs and kings played no part in the selection of successors to the Chewa paramountcy, this being the province of the Mbumba in which Nyangu, the Queen Mother, played and to this day continues to play a pivotal role. Successive Undis, moreover, arbitrated wrangles over boundaries and succession to tributary thrones. Needless to say, Gawa Undi's popularity and success as supreme Chewa leader depended upon how he resolved conflicts in which his sub-chiefs were involved.

---

15 Marwick, "History," speculates that the Phiri clan probably came as invaders.
16 Lyson Chigaga Phiri and Joseph Galeta Chikuta Mbewe, interviews cited.
17 Marwick, "History," p. 389.
18 Langworthy III, "History," p. 26.
19 Interview with Christopher Phiri, Headman, Mnthipa village, Katete, 07 August 2008.

Retaining the loyalty of the subordinate rulers came to rest upon an elaborate network of patronage greased by politics of redistribution. To hold their allegiance, successive Undis garnered and distributed local and imported goods to tributary rulers. This in turn called for maintaining a monopoly over internal and especially external trade with the Portuguese.[20] To this end, Undi, whose successors also inherited his title of Gawa Undi, controlled the trade with the Portuguese well up the 19th century. In this position, he redistributed imported European goods like cloth, beads, and liquor. Lesser chiefs in return paid homage and tribute to the central court at Mano, from where the Chewa overlord channelled the tribute, which included slaves, ivory, iron and gold into the Atlantic trade system in exchange for imported goods.

Tribute and exotic goods thus came to be at the centre-stage of politics of redistribution, and crucial to the expansion of the power, prestige and social status of Kalonga Gawa Undi and of his officials. Since the king strictly controlled access to highly valued trade items and sent part of them to subordinate chiefs in outlying areas, he was able to weld junior rulers to his court in Mozambique. But imported goods were a double-edged sword. Like elsewhere in pre-colonial Africa, they possessed the power either to enhance or to undermine the relations between kings and their subordinates.[21] Indeed, evidence indicates that when the Portuguese began to sell guns directly to Gawa Undi's tributary rulers in the 19th century, they sowed the seed of disruption that eventually undermined the authority and, of course, the power of the Chewa sovereign.[22]

As the overlord and his officials at Mano lost their grip over external trade and goods, rebellious chiefs became more and more politically autonomous. This situation was compounded by the Portuguese and the Arabs, both of whom emasculated the king's monopoly trade through their slave and gold trading activities in the 19th century. In the same century, the Chikunda added to the misfortune of the kingdom either by defeating or conniving with his junior chiefs to establish their own predatory states in areas originally under the jurisdiction of Kalong Gawa Undi. The fate of the Chewa Empire was finally sealed by the arrival of the war-like Ngoni

[20] For a fuller discussion on this topic, see Allen Isaacman and Derek Peterson, "Making the Chikunda: Military Slavery and Ethnicity in Southern Africa, 1750-1900," *International Journal of African Historical Studies* 36, 2 (2003), pp. 257-281.

[21] This point is most poignantly made by Meredith McKittrick, *To Dwell Secure: Generation, Christianity, and Colonialism in Ovamboland* (Portsmouth, NH: Heinemann; Oxford: James Currey and Cape Town: David Philip, 2002), Chapters 1 and 2.

[22] Langworthy III, "History".

under Zwangendaba from South Africa after 1835. The Ngoni ravaged the Chewa in the 1840s, reportedly creating a climate of despondency in Chewa areas.

Ngoni and Chikunda raids drastically reduced the size and power of the Chewa Empire in the second half the 19th century. When David and Charles Livingstone traversed the Chewa territory in the 1850s and 1860s, they recorded that the empire was fast falling apart.[23] By the latter date, most Chewa chiefdoms had either been defeated by the Ngoni under Mpezeni or were continually under a state of siege. However, the reigning Kalonga Gawa Undi in Mozambique seems not to have been defeated by Mpezeni, although he had certainly lost considerable influence among his subjects due to relentless Ngoni raids. Finally, during the 1880s and 1890s, the Chewa kingdom was balkanised between the Portuguese and the British. Later in the 1930s, the incumbent king relocated his capital village to Zambia's Katete district in order to escape the more repressive rule of the Portuguese administration in Mozambique.

Sources and Outline of the Study

This biography draws its materials mainly from primary, secondary and oral sources consulted between 2005 and 2008. Among primary sources are archival documents such as colonial tour and annual reports, press reports, and a handful of letters that Kalonga Gawa Undi X himself wrote to or received from his sub-chiefs and European officials in Zambia's Eastern province. Combined, these sources are frustratingly fragmentary and uneven in terms of their chronological coverage. Although they throw some light on the political thought and praxis of the Paramount Chief between 1953 and 1972, most of these sources are virtually silent on his earlier life and, even more frustratingly, on the decades that immediately preceded his demise in 2004.

In the course of research for this study, an attempt was made to plug the lacunae in documented accounts with data from oral and secondary sources. This involved not merely mining published works but, more importantly, conducting extensive oral interviews with informants—both royals and commoners—who knew or lived with the Paramount Chief prior to his death. These interviews, which commenced in 2005 and ended in 2008, took place mostly in Katete. Only through these oral interviews was it possible to gain some insights into the early and latter life of the

---

[23] See David and Charles Livingstone, *Narrative of an Expedition to the Zambezi and its Tributaries* (New York: Harper and Brothers, 1866), p. 217.

protagonist. But oral sources themselves, like archival documents, are not comprehensive. For, while oral accounts memorialise the virtues of the late traditional ruler, they are, as would be expected, virtually silent on his failings. This is all the more so because Gawa Undi X seems to have been a very popular leader among his subjects. For this reason, chapters in this volume that heavily draw on oral accounts cannot be more than impressionistic.

The second chapter in this volume explores the early life and career of Kalonga Gawa Undi X within the wider contexts of the matrilineal society and colonial rule in which he was born and raised. It insists that although Kalonga Gawa Undi X embraced European education and Christianity, his early life and career were equally informed by his cultural upbringing in Katete. On the other hand, chapter 3 explores transformations in the political thought and praxis of the Chewa overlord between 1953 when he assumed office and 1964 when Zambia attained her independence from Britain. It observes that the Chewa overlord's early years in leadership were marked by his hostility to the independence struggle. The chapter elucidates why he abandoned this posture and became an ardent ally of the anti-colonial movement from 1957 onward. It also illuminates his political praxis through exploring the strategies the sovereign used in combating foreign misrule.

It is misleading to assume that the Chief's contributions to the construction of Zambia were confined to the politics of decolonisation, as popular discourse implies. Chapter 4 shows that Gawa Undi X was as interested in liberating Zambia from vestiges of alien rule as he sought to free its people from the depravations of poverty, both before and after 1964. It further underlines the political tensions that arose between the Chewa potentate and the UNIP-led government in the aftermath of independence. The chapter ends with an examination of why, despite these tensions, Kalonga Gawa Undi X still supported UNIP's call for the one-party system of governance in the early 1970s.

In Chapter 5, we explore the reactions of the Chewa ruler to the country's growing economic and political doldrums that issued from the fall in copper prices, the rise in the cost of oil on the international market after 1972 and, on the political level, from UNIP government's failure to redress the crises coupled with its inability to contain growing corruption and incompetence. The final chapter is an exploration of why Kalonga Gawa Undi X revived the Kulamba ceremony in 1984. The chapter maintains that the Paramount Chief perceived this traditional ceremony as not merely an instrument of cultural preservation but also of regional economic integration. This vision, the chapter concludes, has in recent days been appreciated by leaders in southern Africa.

2

Early Life and Career

Introduction

In the 1960s and 1970s, many analysts including Henry Meebelo and John Illife not infrequently depicted traditional authorities in British Africa as no more than cogs in the wheels of imperial hegemony and domination.[1] According to these theorists, African chiefs were "captured" between serving the conflicting interests of their European masters and those of their own people. Scholars who subscribed to this view asserted that local rulers allied themselves with imperial power because they, the argument continued, were beneficiaries of colonialism, had greater access to Western education than their followers, and were accorded special treatment by their colonial masters. African rulers, therefore, saw their own interests as closely intertwined with those of their white paymasters, rather than those of their subjects.

Several scholars including Giacomo Macola and Samuel Nyangu Chipungu have in more recent decades questioned this perspective.[2] These critics maintain that, ideologically and pragmatically, African rulers in imperial contexts seldom constituted a monolithic category. They, therefore, sometimes held widely contrasting attitudes towards colonial states and even towards their subjects. According to this perspective, some African authorities not only took advantage of colonially-engineered institu-

[1] Henry Meebelo, *Reaction to Colonialism: A Prelude to the Politics of Independence in Northern Zambia, 1893-1939* (Manchester: Manchester University Press, 1971), p. 91; John Illife, "The Age of Improvement and Differentiation," in I. N. Kimambo and A. J. Temu (eds.), *A History of Tanzania* (Nairobi: East African Publishing House, 1969), p. 137. See also Allen Isaacman, "Peasants and Rural Social Protest in Africa," paper commissioned for the Joint ACLS-SSRC Africa Committee presented at the African Studies Association Annual Meeting, 2-6 November 1989, Atlanta, Georgia.

[2] Giacomo Macola, *The Kingdom of Mwata Kazembe: History and Politics in North-Eastern Zambia and Katanga to 1950* (Munster, Hamburg and London: Lit Verlag, 2002), pp 190-193 and Samuel N. Chipungu, "African Leadership under Indirect Rule in Colonial Zambia," in Samuel N. Chipungu ed.), *Guardians in their Time: Experiences of Zambians under Colonial Rule* (London: Macmillan, 1992), pp. 50-73.

tions to bolster their own power and to champion their interests. They also as frequently questioned the excesses of imperial rule while, at the same time, young African royals with Western education sometimes challenged the authority of older, conservative chiefs.[3] Stated in other words, critics of the earlier historiography on indigenous authorities under colonial control perceive them as not accomplices in their own subjugation. To the contrary, these observers regard chiefs as their own social, economic, and political actors, who independently forged varying attitudes, ideas, and practices within the foundry of colonialism. Their ideologies and praxis were thus as heterogeneous as they were often conflicting. In moulding their own ideologies and practices, the traditional ruling elite in colonial Africa confounded the practice of colonial power.

The present chapter seeks to build on these insights through exploring the social, cultural and political dynamics that shaped and were in turn shaped by Obister Chivunga Phiri, who inherited the Chewa throne as Kalonga Gawa Undi X on 3 March 1953. Born in the 1930s at the height of British imperial hegemony in Africa in a matrilineal society that placed a heavy premium on cultural beliefs and practices, the protagonist was as much a product of the colonial space in which he grew up as of his own traditional heritage. The chapter attempts to illuminate how this unusual context moulded his early life and career between 1931 when Obister was born and 1953, when he became a Paramount Chief. It argues that the heir's early experiences were a hybrid of the modern and the traditional. Although he was brought up to be a custodian of Chewa culture, Obister Chivunga Phiri, nonetheless, embraced colonial/missionary education, Christianity, European attire, and other several elements of Western modernity.

It would, however, be grossly misleading to assume that Obister was a simple creation of colonialism, or a blind imitator of European ways of seeing and being. To the contrary, evidence suggests that the future Paramount Chief embraced Christianity and European-style education in accordance with his own needs and existing situation, inscribing both institutions with meanings and uses that neither colonial authorities nor missionaries could fathom or control.[4] Such meanings and functions as the

---

[3] See Macola, *Kingdom of Kazembe*.

[4] This point is informed by Elizabeth Elbourne, "Early Khoisan Uses of Mission Christianity," in Henry Bredekamp and Robert Ross (eds.), *Mission Christianity in South Africa* (Johannesburg: Witwatersrand University Press, 1995); see also Thomas Spear, "Towards the History of African Christianity," in Thomas Spear and Isaria N. Kimambo, *East African Expressions of Christianity* (Oxford: James Currey; Dar es Salaam: Mkuki na Nyota, and Athens: Ohio University Press,

heir imbedded into modern education and Christianity did not always resonate with the expectations of either the authorities or missionaries. The incongruity in beliefs and intentions between Obister Chivunga Phiri and those of colonisers issued from the fact that the former sought to fuse pre-Christian ideas and functions into the European version of Christianity and education. He also believed, as shown in the next chapter, that imperial institutions in Africa could be refashioned to champion the welfare of the subjects of empire, and also, ironically, to undercut imperial subjugation or domination. His endeavour to promote the interests of his people through colonial institutions insulates him from the all-too-familiar discourse that caricatures indigenous authorities in Africa as accomplices who acquiesced in their own domination and that of their followers.

Obister Chivunga Phiri's Early Life

Reconstructing the early life history of Kalonga Gawa Undi X *né* Obister Chivunga Phiri is attended by imponderable difficulties because of the fragmentary nature of the evidence available to the historian. Save for a speech he himself delivered in 2003 during the golden jubilee of his ascension to the Chewa throne and a handful of letters he sent to or received from subordinate chiefs and colonial functionaries in which one may glean his ideas and childhood experiences, the protagonist left no detailed documented account of his life. Thus, what is known about his early life derives mostly from the speech itself; scanty archival documents and the oral accounts of informants who lived with him before his death in 2004.[5] Neither of these sources is unproblematic. When Kalonga Gawa Undi X made the speech in 2003, he was already seventy-two years old and in poor health. This may have deeply influenced what he recollected of his earlier life. On the other hand, documentary accounts (including his letters) that shed light on the Paramount Chief's life are both fragmentary and scanty. At the same time, oral testimonies tend to extol his accomplishments, while minimising his failures. Given all these limitations the picture of the early life, ideologies and experiences of the Chewa sovereign can only at best be impressionistic.

According to oral testimony, Obister Chivunga Phiri was born to Chikakozi Phiri and Msenya Phiri at Chambobo village near the present-day Zambia-Mozambique border on January 1, 1931.[6] The only son in his family,

1999), pp. 3-24.

[5] Kalonga Gawa Undi X, "Speech during the Golden Jubilee Celebrations," Mkaika Traditional Headquarters, Katete, 3 March 2003." In this study the names Obister Chivunga Phiri and Kalonga Gawa Undi X are used interchangeably

he spent his first years at Mnthipa village, Katete district, in Zambia's Eastern province with his mother, father and his uncle Kalonga Gawa Undi IX Chimphungu. The other close kinsfolk with whom the heir spent his early childhood were his mother's sister named Ndalama, whose son, Chisaka, was older than Obister and also eligible to ascend the Chewa throne. As Chikakozi was older than Ndalama, however, her son, Obister Chivunga Phiri, was, in keeping with Chewa customary law of succession, more qualified for the throne than his cousin, Chisaka. At Mnthipa village, both boys came under the tutelage of their uncle, Gawa Undi IX Chimphungu, whose influence profoundly shaped Obister's early education and career. It was from Chimphungu that Obister Chivunga Phiri would also inherit the Chewa throne as Gawa Undi X on 3 March 1953.[7]

Comparatively speaking, there is little information about the heir's father, Msenya Phiri. This may be appreciated against a brief backcloth of the society in which the future sovereign grew up. Chewa society is organised around a matrilineal system of descent. Like among other related social formations in Central Africa, familial identity, land, and inheritance among the Chewa are transmitted via the mother's line, with family property, and children being under the control of her lineage. Moreover, the Chewa traditionally practise virilocal marriages. This means that newly married wives leave their natal areas to live in the villages of their husbands. Conflictingly, however, their offspring especially sons traditionally tended to live in their maternal uncles' villages, to which their mothers and sisters also returned when divorced or widowed. Under this social arrangement, maternal uncles unsurprisingly enjoyed greater domestic authority and power over their sisters' children than fathers. To all intents and purposes, uncles were responsible for raising nephews and, in some cases, nieces. That we know so little about Obister's father issued from the fact that Kalonga Gawa Undi IX Chimphungu played a more important role than Msenya Phiri in the upbringing of his nephew and in moulding his early life, career, and character.

The community in which our protagonist was raised was not immune from the social tensions characteristic of all societies organised on the

---

6 Interview with Lyson Chigaga Phiri, Headman and Senior Advisor to Kalonga Gawa Undi, Mwanzaulungu Village, Katete, 6 August 2008.

7 Much of the data on the early life of Kalonga Gawa Undi X issues from Interviews with Lydia Nkhoma and Ireena Phiri, Cousins of Kalonga Gawa Undi X, Mkaika Palace, Katete, 12 Novemeber 2007; Lyson Chigaga Phiri, interview cited; Kamlendo Phiri, Peasant farmer, Mnthipa Village, 7 August 2008; Kafuwa Yobe Chimberekero, Headman, Kafumbwe Basic School, 8 August 2008 . See also Kalonga Gawa Undi X, Speech during Golden Jubilee in 2003," Mkaika Palace, Katete, 03 March 2003. ."

contradictory principles of matrilineality and virilocality. These principles brought people into certain relationships but opposed them in others. This inevitably spawned conflicts of loyalties, a situation that has been observed in other similarly organised societies.[8] Given virilocal marriages, male uterine siblings, for example, were brought together in matrikin villages but only at the cost of separating them from their sisters and sister's sons, their natural heirs. In the same vein, matrilineal descent coupled with

Photo 1 Chewa Traditional rulers under colonial rule. Kalonga Gawa Undi X is third from left in the front row. Courtesy of National Archives of Zambia.

[8] There is abundant literature on this topic. See Victor Turner, *Schism and Continuity in an African Society: A Study of Ndembu Village Life* (Manchester: Manchester University Press, 1957); *The Drums of Affliction: A Study of Religious Processes among the Ndembu of Zambia* (Oxford: Oxford University Press, 1969); The Forest of Symbols: Aspects of Ndembu Ritual (Ithaca, N.Y.: Cornell University Press, 1967); *Revelation and Divination in Ndembu Ritual* (Ithaca, N.Y. and London: Cornell University Press, 1975). For studies that question Turner's perspectives, see James Anthony Pritchett, "Change and Continuity in an African Society: "The Kanongesha Lunda of Mwinilunga, Zambia," (unpublished doctoral dissertation, Harvard University, 1989); Lunda-Ndembu: *Style, Change and Social Transformation in South Central Africa* (Madison: The University of Wisconsin Press, 2001); *Friends for Life, Friends for Death: Cohorts and Consciousness among the Lunda-Ndembu* (Charlottesville and London: Virginia University Press, 2007); Walima T. Kalusa, "Disease and the Remaking of Missionary Medicine in Colonial North-Western Zambia: A Case of Mwinilunga District, 1902-1964," (unpublished doctoral dissertation, Johns Hopkins University, 2003); Boris Wastiau, "Mahamba: The Transforming Arts of Spirit Possession among the Luvale-Speaking People of the Upper Zambezi," (unpublished doctoral dissertation, University of East Anglia, 1997); Sonia Silva "Vicarious Selves: Divination Baskets and Angola Refugees in Zambia," (unpublished doctoral dissertation, Indiana University, 1999).

virilocal marriages created fault lines and tensions between male uterine groups in adjacent generations, between the descendants of the father's wife, and descendants of father's sisters, as well as between descendants of uterine sisters.[9]

Within the context of Chewa matrilineal society, competing loyalties and resultant tensions within and between these social categories were unavoidable. Male uterine siblings competed for the loyalty of their sisters and sister's offspring, without whose support one could not attain the chiefly office. Similarly, uncles' control over their sisters' children also sometimes drew them into conflicts with their brothers-in-law and male siblings as they competed to assert control over their sisters' offspring. Thus, like in other matrilineal social formations, the Chewa social organisation was inherently unstable politically and socially.

In this situation, it is no surprise that men aspiring for either political office or influence needed to possess more than just royal blood in their veins. They had to demonstrate the ability to attract to their villages their sisters and sister's children in the face of virilocal marriages which took females and their offspring away from matrikin villages after women married. The need to win over the support of sisters, their offspring, and male relations called for mastery of a host of social and political skills essential to both attracting followers and, more significantly, retaining their loyalty. The Chewa chief or headman worth his position, therefore, had to be a skilful negotiator, an arbitrator capable of judging cases with impartiality. He further needed to be an intermediary who communed with the ancestors to safeguard the welfare of his subjects.[10] It goes without saying that success in performing these onerous functions required sound knowledge of local customary law, rituals, history, and of the boundaries between various chiefdoms. By all accounts, Kalonga Gawa Undi IX Chimphungu, under whose tutelage young Obister Chivunga Phiri received his informal education, possessed the essential skills, attributes, and qualities expected of a Chewa traditional ruler.[11] Reportedly an acclaimed authority on Chewa history, culture, and law, Kalonga Gawa Undi IX Chimphungu is memorialised among his descendants as a highly skilled political, legal, and social actor. It may have been for this reason that the Paramount Chief attracted to his capital village at Mnthipa a huge following, including the

---

[9] Pritchett, "Change and Continuity".

[10] See NAZ EP 1/1/12, D.B. Hall, Secretary of Native Affairs to Provincial Commissioners, 25 January 1958.

[11] Lydia Nkhoma and Ireena Phiri, interview cited.

nuclear and extended family of his future successor.[12]

At Mnthipa village, young Obister often observed uncle Chimphungu and his councillors as they arbitrated their subjects' disputes. It is recalled that when court was in session, Kalonga Gawa Undi IX Chipumhungu seldom spoke but allowed both the plaintiff and defendant to say all they had to say, all the while intently listening to them. Once they had spoken, the potentate, assisted by his councillors, passed his verdict. Legend has it that he was sometimes harsh with the guilty party but more often lenient in his judgements in the expectation that those found guilty would not commit crimes again. In judging cases brought before him, Chimphungu allegedly relied not on his councillors' advice alone. It is said that he also depended on local customs, profusely quoting Chewa proverbs to punctuate the sentences he meted out to the guilty and to the innocent. For all this, the overlord, like his nephew after him, was revered among his followers.[13]

Kalonga Gawa Undi IX Chimphungu evidently left a lasting impact on young Obister, to whom he gave the name Chivunga.[14] In allowing the heir to observe court proceedings at Mnthipa village, the older ruler drilled into his charge traditional leadership qualities together with the legal and spiritual responsibilities of the Chewa overlord. This apparently equipped young Obister with juridical knowledge that later enabled him to become an accomplished arbitrator in his subjects' disputes. Like Chimphungu, Kalonga Gawa Undi X would later earn for himself a reputation as an impartial mediator. This view was shared not among his subjects alone; it was also documented by colonial authorities.[15]

Besides imbibing the legal expertise of his uncle, Obister Chivunga Phiri seems to have also acquired from his benefactor insights into and knowledge of local customs, history, rituals, and of chiefly boundaries. All this apparently left in him a deep devotion to Chewa folklore, history, and traditions that remained with him throughout his life.[16] The fact that Kalonga Gawa Undi X resuscitated the Kulamba ceremony in 1984 after it had been in abeyance for fifty years clearly attests to the truism in this observation.[17] Finally, oral accounts indicate that it was from Chimphungu

[12] Lyson Chigaga Phiri Interview cited.

[13] Lydia Nkhoma and Ireena Phiri, interview cited. In traditional African society, Chimphungu's legal expertise was universally recognised as the hallmark of wisdom. See Kenneth Bradley, *Once a District Officer* (New York: St Martin's Press, 1966).

[14] Kalonga Gawa Undi X, "Speech".

[15] See NAZ EP 1/1/12, Paramount Chief Undi to District Commissioner (DC), Fort Jameson, 18 November 1963. On the same file, see P.M. Lawson to DC, Fort Jameson, 19 November 1963.

[16] Mama Nyangu and Lyson Chigaga Phiri, interviews cited.

[17] See President Levy Patrick Mwanawasa, "Speech by His Excellency the President of the Republic

that the protégé learned how to win the loyalty of his subjects, how to maintain good relations with subordinate chiefs, and how to retain his followers' respect, thus ensuring social and political tranquillity and harmony.[18]

By the time Kalonga Gawa Undi IX Chimphungu died in 1952, he had, therefore, already left no small influence over his successor. But even before the benefactor passed away, other forces that would equally contribute to moulding his nephew's ideologies and practices were swiftly sweeping across the political, cultural, economic, and social landscape in Central Africa. As early as the 1930s, the British were consolidating the system of Indirect Rule throughout their African domain. Simply defined, Indirect Rule was a system through which British authorities imposed their political, social, and economic sway over the colonised and made economic demands on them through their own traditional rulers and institutions.[19] African traditional authorities, under this system of imperial control, served as administrative auxiliaries. Their responsibilities included collecting tax from their subjects, maintaining law and order, and enforcing the directives of the colonial state in areas under their jurisdiction.[20] In practical terms, however, chiefs enjoyed no real political power. They were meant to be no more than salaried functionaries operating at the lower echelons of the imperial administration.

To improve the administrative efficiency of African traditional rulers and to encourage their participation in government-sponsored programmes, British authorities in colonial Zambia began in the 1920s to encourage chiefs and/or chief designates to various thrones in the territory to receive Western education, preferably at government-run schools.[21] Colonial authorities envisaged that African rulers with Western-style education would easily acquire knowledge of modern administration, besides imbibing European values. In this way, they would become beacons of Enlightenment, dispersing modern values and undermining "pagan" cul-

---

of Zambia Mr Levy Patrick Mwanawasa, SC, on the Occasion of the 2007 Kulamba Traditional Ceremony of the Chewa People of Malawi, Mozambique and Zambia on the 25th August, 2007 at Mkaika Palace in Katete."

[18] Kamlendo Phiri, Peasant Farmer, Mnthipa Village, 7 August 2008; Lyson Chigaga, interview cited.

[19] A recent sophisticated exploration of the Indirect Rule in British Africa is Mahmood Mamdani, *Citizen and Subject: Contemporary Africa and the Legacy of Late Colonialism* (Princeton, New Jersey: Princeton University Press, 1996. See also Macola, *Kingdom of Kazembe*.

[20] For a fuller treatment of this topic, see Kusum Datta, "The Policy of Indirect Rule in Northern Rhodesia (Zambia), 1924-1953," PhD dissertation: University of London, 1976 and Ben C. Kakoma, "Colonial Administration in Northern Rhodesia: A Case Study of Administration in Mwinilunga District, 1900-1939," MA dissertation: University of Auckland, 1977.

[21] See Macola, *Kingdom of Kazembe*, pp. 213-214.

ture in the "Dark Continent".[22] In Zambia's Eastern province, as elsewhere in British Africa, this policy found pragmatic expression in the agility with which colonial authorities supplanted uneducated traditional authorities with Western educated chiefs from the 1930s onwards.[23]

In this context, it is unsurprising that Kalonga Gawa Undi IX Chimphungu and other members of the Chewa royal family unanimously agreed to send both Obister Chivunga Phiri and Chisaka to Catholic mission schools first at Mnthipa village towards the end of the 1930s and later at Naviruli in Katete district. Young Obister seems to have progressed fairly rapidly in school. For at the age of eighteen years in 1949, he was admitted as a trainee teacher to Chalimbana Teachers Training College in Lusaka.[24] But when his cousin, Chisaka, the only other heir, was killed in a motorcycle accident at Chassa in Zambia's Petauke district in the same year, the royal family promptly withdrew Obister from the college lest he, too, met a similar fate. Kalonga Gawa Undi X would later recall with deep regret the impact Chisaka's untimely death had on the surviving heir's education:

> I suffered a big educational setback when Chisaka was run over by a motorcycle driven by a Catholic Missionary at Chassa Secondary School turn off and died in the year 1949. Uncle Chimphungu and indeed the entire family in agreement decided to withdraw me from [my] academic pursuit at Chalimbana Teacher's College for fear of me meeting [a similar] calamity.[25]

Withdrawn from college, the future Chewa Paramount Chief returned to Katete district. This posed a major barrier to his quest for post-primary education, as such opportunities in the district and the Eastern province as a whole were extremely limited. "It is impossible," lamented one colonial functionary in the province as late as 1951, "to feel confident that education is making progress in this area."[26] A year later, the same officer attributed this situation to the indifference of the colonial government towards African education in the area.[27]

But the heir was apparently not deterred by the dearth of post-primary education in the province. Not long after he was withdrawn from college,

---

[22] See Frederick Cooper, *Decolonization and African Society: The Labor Question in French and British Africa* (Cambridge: Cambridge University Press, 1996), p. 213. But see also Sara S. Berry, *Chiefs Know their Boundaries: Essays on Property, Power and the Past in Asante, 1896-1996* (Portsmouth, NH: Heinemann; Oxford: James Currey and Cape Town: David Philip, 2001), p. 36.

[23] NAZ SEC2/706, H. H. Thomson, District Officer, Katete Tour Report No. 2, 1952

[24] Kalonga Gawa Undi X, "Speech".

[25] Kalonga Gawa Undi X, "Speech".

[26] NAZ SEC2/705, Katete Tour Report No. 2 of 1951.

[27] NAZ SEC2/706, Katete Tour Report No. 4 of 1952.

he started a correspondence course in the early 1950s with a college in either colonial Zimbabwe or South Africa.[28] In subsequent years, he also repeatedly implored his sub-chiefs and their subjects to send as many children as could be accommodated in the few available schools in Eastern province, a point to which we shall return in the next chapter. It is most unlikely, though, that Kalonga Gawa Undi X's penchant for Western education was only inspired by the colonisers' drive to improve the administrative efficiency of African chiefs. This view finds support in the fact that his correspondence programme, for which he himself paid from his pocket, included no courses in colonial administration or leadership training.[29] Most prominent among the subjects the Chief pursued in the correspondence course was English. Oral accounts indicate that Kalonga Gawa Undi X earnestly sought to become proficient in the English language, and he evidently spent many years trying to perfect his command of the language.[30] By the late 1950s and the early 1960s, the traditional ruler indeed wrote and spoke fairly passable English.[31]

It is not too difficult to comprehend why the young ruler came to place so great an emphasis on the English language and literacy. Obister Chivunga Phiri grew up in a world where English and literacy were indisputably becoming an important source of power, authority and influence. Proficiency in written and spoken English not only signalled one's mastery of the imperial world and of its technologies. It also enabled those who acquired it to manage old and new concerns in a rapidly changing world. Armed with English, one could speak back to the coloniser in this language of empire, and on equal terms.[32] Learning the language was thus an essential step colonial subjects had to take to enter what Jean and John Comarrof have aptly called the "long conversation" with the coloniser.[33] English was the bargaining chip by which Africans and other people under British rule could and did defend their own interests in the face of indifferent rulers.

There is ample archival evidence to suggest that Obister Chivunga

---

[28] Mama Nyangu, interview cited. The informant was not certain as to where the college was located.
[29] Kalonga Gawa Undi X later received leadership training at Torquay in Britain. See next chapter.
[30] Interview with Alick Chafunya Phiri, Headman, Kafumbwe Village, 8 August 2008.
[31] This assessment is based on a few letters the chief wrote in English to fellow chiefs and colonial authorities and the speeches he made as President of the House of Chiefs between the late 1960s and 1970s. Alick Chafunya Phiri, interview cited.
[32] For an interesting article on this topic, see Amanda D. Kemp and Robert Trent Vinson, "'Poking Holes in the Sky': Professor James Thaele, American Negroes, and Modernity in Segregationist South Africa," *African Studies Review* 43, 1 (2000), pp. 141-159.
[33] Jean Comaroff and John Comaroff, *Of Revelation and Revolution: Christianity, Colonialsim and Consciousness in South Africa* Vol. One (Chicago and London: The University of Chicago Press, 1991).

Phiri was not slow to deploy his knowledge of English to come to terms with the rapidly changing world, as well as to redress both new and old problems. This is plainly evidenced by the letters he wrote as Chief Designate to the District Commissioner (DC) at Fort Jameson (now Chipata) and to Chewa-speaking chiefs in Malawi in 1952 to counteract stiff opposition to his enthronement from especially the Chewa Chief, Mkanda Mateyo. This chief strongly objected to being treated as junior to Kalonga Gawa Undi and refused to recognise Obister Chivunga Phiri as the rightful heir to the Chewa throne. Even more ominously, the former called for the abolition of the Undi Paramountcy on the ground that it did not exist prior to British colonialism.[34]

In the letters Obister Chivunga Phiri penned in English to defend his own claim to the throne, he dismissed the grounds of his rival as not only baseless but also devoid of popular support among other Chewa chiefs.[35] Another letter, in which the heir responded to the DC's castigation of how Obister had settled a marital dispute, is equally revealing. In the letter written in English on 7th August 1952, the Chief Designate reminded the DC in Chipata that in mediating his subjects' marriage wrangles, the heir relied on Africa matrimonial customs, and not on British colonial laws.[36] Plainly, the future Paramount Chief employed English to champion his claim to the highest Chewa chiefly office, and, equally importantly, to repudiate imperial interventions in local customs.

As many scholars have remarked of local elites in the British Empire generally, Obister Chivunga Phiri was further not unaware that mastery of the language of the coloniser definitively mapped the road to raising one's social standing through pursuing a career in the unfolding colonial economy.[37] Indeed, it was because of his command of English and writing skills that he served as Chimphungu's court clerk between 1950 and 1952, as the secretary of the Council of Chiefs in Eastern Province in 1967, and,

---

[34] M.G. Marwick, "History and Tradition in East Central Africa through the Eyes of the Northern Rhodesia Chewa," *Journal of African History* 4, 3 (1963), p. 389.

[35] National Archives of Zambia (hereinafter NAZ) EP4/7/13, Obister Chivunga Undi to DC, 12 November 1952; see also NAZ EP4/7/13, Alexander Mbewa to DC, Fort Jameson, 17 January 1953; NAZ EP 4/7/13, K.A.G.J. Nyanda Nthuru to DC, 18 December 1952.

[36] NAZ EP4/7/13, Paramount Chief Undi to District Commissioner, Fort Jameson, 7 August 1952.

[37] See Fay Gadsden, "Education and Society in Colonial Zambia," in Chipungu (ed.), *Guardians in their Time*, pp. 97-125; John Mwanakatwe, *The Growth of Education in Zambia since Independence* (Lusaka: Oxford University Press, 1974); Peter Snelson, *Educational Development in Northern Rhodesia, 1883-1945* (Lusaka: Neczam, 1974); A.K Msiko and Elizabeth C. Mumba, "A Historical Perspective of Adult Education in Zambia," in H.J. Msango, E.C. Mumba, and A.L. Sikwibele (eds.), *Selected Topics in Philosophy and Education 1* (Lusaka: The University of Zambia Press, 2000), pp. 120-129.

respectively, as Vice-Chairman and Chairman of the House of Chiefs from 1965 to 1967 and from 1968 to 1981.[38] Most significantly, his knowledge of the language enabled him to play a no minor role in the constitutional talks both at home and overseas in the 1950s and 1960s. It was through these debates that Africans in colonial Zambia eventually broke the backbone of British hegemony and wrested power from unwilling colonisers in 1964.

To Kalonga Gawa Undi X, therefore, Western education with its allied English language was more than just a medium of enhancing African chiefs' administrative efficiency, as colonial rulers intended. Nor was it a vehicle of cultural destruction, as missionaries hoped. With the benefit of hindsight, the Chief perceived European education and the English language as an instrument of entitlement by which imperial subjects could contest the power of indifferent colonisers. It is little wonder, then, that after Kalonga Gawa Undi X joined the anti-colonial fray in the late 1950s, he, as already noted, deployed the imperial language to challenge British hegemony and to negotiate for independence both at home and in Britain, where the Chief took an active part in constitutional debates.[39]

If the Chewa Paramount Chief's perception of colonial education with its associated English language diametrically diverged from the intentions and expectations of the agents of the British Empire in Africa, so did his conception and praxis of Christianity. It is difficult to assign a precise date to when the indigenous ruler embraced Christianity. It is certain, however, that young Obister converted to Christianity prior to his ascendancy to the Chewa throne when he attended one of the two Catholic schools noted earlier. His conversion was probably encouraged by Monsignor Bishop Firmin Courtemanche. Like most other European missionaries to Africa, Bishop Courtemanche, who presided over the Chipata diocese in eastern Zambia from 1946 to 1971, held that Africans could easily be drawn to Christianity once their local rulers converted to the faith. He envisaged that Christian chiefs would become missionaries' allies in undermining African "pagan" culture. It may be for this reason that the Catholic Bishop main-

---

[38] Gawa Undi X, "Speech"; NAZ EP1/1/54, B.M. Bwalya, Resident Secretary, to Clerk of the House of Chiefs, 31 December 1965

[39] These insights are inspired by Derek R. Peterson, *Creative Writing: Translation, Book-Keeping, and the Work of Imagination in Colonial Kenya* (Portsmouth, NH: Heinemann, 2004; Patrick Harries, "Missionaries, Marxists, and Magic: Power and the Politics of Literacy in South-East Africa," *Journal of Southern African Studies* 23, 3 (2001), pp. 405-427. See also his *Butterflies and Barbarians: Swiss Missionaries and Systems of Knowledge in South-East Africa* (Oxford: James Currey; Harare: Weaver; Johannesburg: Wits University Press and Athens: Ohio University Press, 2007), Chapter 6, and *Work, Culture, and Identity: Migrant Laborers in Mozambique and South Africa, c. 1860-1910* (Portsmouth NH: Heinemann; Johannesburg: Witwatersrand University Press and London, 1994).

tained a life-long relationship with the Chewa Paramount Chief.[40]

There are a number of factors that suggest that Kalonga Gawa Undi X was deeply devoted to the Christian faith. Firstly, he unfailingly always endorsed the extension of Catholic land leases in Eastern province when they expired.[41] Secondly, the Paramount Chief, in his own words, had a "burning desire" to meet the Pope, the spiritual head of the Catholic Church. To this end, the Chewa ruler successfully asked Bishop Courtemanche to make arrangements so that the traditional ruler could stopover in the Vatican on his return journey to colonial Zambia after his first visit to England in the 1950s. As Kalonga Gawa Undi X himself later recalled, he for many years had:

> a burning desire to have an audience with the Holy Father, his holiness POPE PIUS XII IN ROME. I was corresponding with the then Fort Jameson DIOCESE, his Lordship Bishop COURTEMANCHE to pave the way for the visit to the Vatican. By those arrangements, it was made possible for me to do so. On my way from Britain, [I] stopped over in ROME.[42]

The Paramount Chief was unable to meet the Pope personally. Nevertheless, he enthusiastically received blessings from the Catholic leader's balcony. For many years to come, the Chief regaled his admiring subjects with recollections of his experiences in Rome and the Vatican:

> I was privileged to be taken round the VATICAN and ST. PETER'S SQUARE[.] [A]lthough it was not possible for me to meet the POPE personally [I] received his blessings from the balcony of CASTLE GONDOF where the Pope was. I was taken on the conducted tour of the CITY OF ROME including CATACOMBS in the city... [and] ST. PETER'S CATHEDRAL. I also managed to travel along the APIAN WAY which road PETER the Apostle used to run away from ROME in fear of persecution.... In the process, the Apostle criss-crossed the LORD JESUS CHRIST. PETER recognised the face of JESUS and asked him where he was heading to. In reply, Jesus said he was going to ROME to die for the second time because he (PETER) was running away from being his witness. PETER immediately returned to ROME in heavy tears accepting to later meet his death for the propagation of the faith.[43]

---

[40] For more details about Bishop Courtemanche, see Walima T. Kalusa, "From an Agency of Cultural Destruction to an Agency of Public Health: Transformations in Catholic Missionary Medicine in Post-Colonial Zambia, 1964-1982," paper presented at the Joint Conference held in Freiburg, Germany and Basel, Switzerland, 14-17 May 2008.

[41] NAZ EP1/1/19, District Commissioner to Acting Permanent Secretary, Ministry of Native Affairs, 29 August 1963. See also D.C. Clough , District Commissioner, to Acting Provincial Commissioner 23 July 1963.

[42] Kalonga Gawa Undi X, "Speech". Capital letters are in the original document.

[43] Kalonga Gawa Undi X, "Speech".

These reminiscences testify to the Chewa overlord's commitment to Christianity. They further suggest that he had a deep understanding of the early history of the Catholic Church. Indeed, his faith in Catholicism outlived colonialism. This is plainly demonstrated by the marathon religious pilgrimage the Paramount Chief made in 1975. This pilgrimage took him to Rome, to the Vatican (where he met Pope VI), to Lourdes in France, believed to be the place where the Virgin Mary spoke to Bernadette, and, finally, to the Holy Land.[44] In addition, as late as 2003, Kalonga Gawa Undi X himself would declare that he was "brought up by the Catholic Church."[45]

But his commitment to Christianity did not come without complications. As the spiritual head of the Chewa nation, the traditional ruler could not completely detach himself from pre-existing religious, rituals, and practices that clearly defined the office of the Chewa Paramountcy but which Catholic missionaries paradoxically condemned as the fortress of African "paganism". As Chief Designate, Obister, for example, had to and did inherit his late uncle's youngest wife in keeping with local customs of succession. Nor could Kalonga Gawa Undi X jettison such ritual dances as the Gule Wamkulu performed at the installation ceremony of each new Chewa chief, the performers of which were/are believed to emerge from graves.[46] His direct or indirect involvement in these rituals subverted European missionary discourse that regarded wife inheritance and traditional ceremonies in Africa with deep scorn.[47]

Unlike European evangelists, our protagonist did not condemn polygamy, a widely recognised practice among his people. By the same token, he could not stand aloof from installing sub-chiefs. One of the most important tasks of the Chewa overlord, the installation of new subordinate rulers was a highly ritualised affair. It involved, inter alia, invoking the blessings of past chiefs, pouring libations to the living dead, and beseeching them to ensure the welfare of the living. Like his predecessors who never converted to Christianity, Kalonga Gawa Undi X participated in these rituals, notwithstanding that Catholic missionaries dismissed them as the fortress of "paganism". Finally, although the potentate's adherence to Christianity spanned several decades, it was only two years before his death in 2004 that he accepted to be baptised.[48]

---

44 Ibid.
45 Ibid.
46 Ibid.
47 Lyson Chigaga Phiri and Mama Nyangu, interviews cited.

It may be inferred from the foregoing that Kalonga Gawa Undi X, who is remembered to have been "at ease with Christianity as much as he was with his traditional heritage", filtered Christianity through pre-existing religious knowledge and inscribed the new faith with local meanings, idioms, and uses.[49] During installation rituals, he allegedly invoked the blessings of his predecessors with the same facility that he beseeched the Christian God to bless the fertility of the land and of its people.[50] But the Chief did more. Just as he strongly urged his subjects to embrace Western education, so did he encourage them to turn to Christianity. Indeed, after he ascended the throne in 1953, the new ruler assiduously endeavoured to fill Native Authorities under his sway with chiefs and councillors who had turned to the new faith. From this perspective, it can be argued that the ruler wittingly or unwittingly transformed Christianity into a *modus operandi* for those aspiring to climb to the chiefly office. Put in other words, Kalonga Gawa Undi X used his new faith to confer legitimacy and new social identity upon his subordinate chiefs. He thus reconfigured Christianity into an instrument for addressing new and old concerns, and ultimately recreating local politics, culture, and identity.[51]

The facility with which the traditional ruler drew on Christian and pre-existing religious cosmologies indicates that he did not draw a thick line between the new faith and Chewa religious beliefs. Unlike European missionaries who perceived Christianity as a means by which they would sweep away all non-Western religious paradigms and recreate the African society in their own image, the traditional ruler embraced Christianity without completely rejecting local religious and cultural forms and beliefs. To the contrary, Kalonga Gawa Undi X made sense of the alien religion through pre-existing religious idioms and praxis. In so doing, he re-interpreted Christianity, investing it with meanings that white missionaries could neither fathom nor prevent. By invoking the Christian God in enthronement rituals, the Chief also conferred new functions upon the new religion, thereby contributing to its domestication, indigenisation and popularisation.[52] The Paramount Chief thus wittingly or unwittingly partic-

---

[48] Lyson Chigag Phiri, interview cited.

[49] Ibid.

[50] Ibid.

[51] This situation was replicated by other traditional authorities who converted to Christianity in other parts of Africa and beyond before and after the 19th and 20th centuries. See, for example, Paul Stuart Landau, *The Realm of the Word: Language, Gender, and Christianity in a Southern African Kingdom* (Portsmouth NH; Heinemann; Cape Town: David Philip, and London: James Currey, 1995). See also Emmanuel Akyeampong, "Christianity, Modernity and the Weight of Tradition in the Life of Asantehene Agyeman Prempeh I, c. 1888-1931," *Africa* 69, 2 (1999), pp. 279-311.

ipated in the global phenomenon in which the subjects of the European empire in the 19th and 20th centuries appropriated Western beliefs, idioms, and technologies but simultaneously re-interpreted them in order to fit them in the local cultural logic and practices. As a corollary, the potentate subverted the missionary hegemonic crusade that sought to subdue all forms of non-Western culture in order to render colonial subjects more amenable to European social, economic, cultural and political subjugation.[53]

Conclusion

Kalonga Gawa Undi X Obister Chivunga Phiri's early life, beliefs and career were a hybrid of the traditional and the modern. Raised in a matrilineal society at the peak of British hegemony in pre-independent Zambia, his experiences were as much influenced by the social organisation in which Kalonga Gawa Undi X grew up as they were informed by colonialism, Western education and Christianity. He not only imbibed local cultural values that define(d) the Chewa society and the Chewa chiefly office. The traditional ruler also used them as a framework through which he comprehended and came to terms with Christianity and modernity. Thus, unlike Western agents of the British empire who saw Western education and Christianity as instruments of cultural annihilation in Africa, Kalonga Gawa Undi X invested in both institutions new meanings and functions informed by local culture and logic. In this way, he turned Christianity and European-style education into a vehicle through which he and his people reconfigured their own beliefs, identity, and power without doing away with their own cultural roots and practices. In this way, the sovereign subverted the imperial agenda whose architects sought to recreate the African society according to Western values and precepts. That Kalonga Gawa Undi X transformed colonial institutions to his own advantage became even clearer in the late 1950s when he enlisted in the anti-colonial

---

52 This point is informed by Kalusa, "Remaking Missionary Medicine," p. 123.

53 There is a fast growing body of literature on issues raised here. See Thomas Spear, "Towards the History of African Christianity," in Thomas Spear and Isaria N. Kimambo (eds.), *East African Expression of Christianity* (Oxford: James Currey; Walima T. Kalusa , "Language, Medical Auxiliaries, and the Re-Interpretation of Missionary Medicine in Colonial Mwinilunga, 1922-51," *Journal of Eastern African History* 1, 1 (2007), pp. 57-78; Vicente L. Rafael, *Contracting Colonialism: Translation and Christian Conversion in Tagalog Society Under Early Spanish Rule* (Durham and London: Duke University Press, 1993; Landau, *Realm of the Word*; Pier M. Larson, "'Capacities and Modes of Thinking': Intellectual Engagements and Subaltern Hegemony in the Early Malagasy Christianity," *American Historical Review* 102, 4 (1997), pp. 969-1002; David Maxwell, *Christians and Chiefs: A Social History of the Hwesa People c. 1870s-1990s* (London: Edinburg University Press, 1999 and his "The Spirit and the Scapular: Pentecostal and Catholic Interactions in Northern Nyanga District, Zimbabwe in the 1950s and 1960s," *Journal of Southern African Studies* 23, 2 (1997), pp. 283-300.

struggle and began to contest British hegemony through Native Authorities and other colonially-inspired institutions. Ironically, it was through these same institutions that British authorities hoped to proscribe African nationalism in colonial Zambia. It is to this story that the next chapter turns.

3

THE QUEST FOR FREEDOM

In this country of ours [Kalonga] Gawa Undi [X] did a great job because he helped
in fighting for independence to get back this country. He is the one who suffered
going to England to negotiate with whites for us to get independence. That [was
his] greatest achievement.... We are in power because of Gawa Undi.[1]

Introduction

It is widely acknowledged in popular discourse that Obister Chivunga
Phiri, who at the age of twenty-two years ascended the Chewa throne as
Kalonga Gawa Undi X in 1953 in Zambia's Eastern Province, was a nationalist freedom fighter.[2] This acknowledgement derives not only from the fact
that in the late 1950s the Paramount Chief enlisted in nationalist struggle
for black majority rule first under the banner of the African National
Congress (ANC) and later the United National Independence Party (UNIP).
It also emanates from the fact that Paramount Chief actively took part in the
1958 and 1960 constitutional talks both in Lusaka and London. These talks
culminated in the dissolution of the Federation of Rhodesia and Nyasaland
in 1963 and ultimately in the country's liberation from British political
hegemony in 1964.

The observation that Kalonga Gawa Undi X took part in constitutional
negotiations out of which independent Zambia emerged is beyond re-
proach. But approaching his involvement in the nationalist struggle from
the vantage point of constitutional debates alone creates the impression
that the traditional ruler's contribution to the construction of modern Zambia (formerly Northern Rhodesia) was restricted to the politics of decolonisation. This approach is misleading in two main ways. First, the approach

---

1 Interview with Mama Nyangu [Queen Mother to Kalonga Gawa Undi], Mkaika Palace, Katete, 12
November 2005.
2 Listard Elifala Chambuli Banda, *The Chewa Kingdom* (Lusaka: Desert Enterprises Limited, 2002),
p. 5.

masks the social, economic, and political dynamics that propelled him to enlist in the nationalist movement in the late 1950s and obscures shifts in the Chief's political thought. There are strong indications that in the earliest years of his reign, Kalonga Gawa Undi X maintained a distance from the anti-colonial drama partly due the authoritarian brand of the nationalism espoused by the African National Congress and the United National Independence Party. Indeed, it was not until the late 1950s that the young ruler joined the anti-colonial fray. Until then, he preferred to carry out his chiefly duties within the realm of colonial institutions probably because the potentate felt that doing so offered the best opportunity to ameliorate the socio-economic welfare of his people.

Second, the approach in question hardly illustrates what strategy the traditional ruler pursued against British political ascendancy once he enlisted in the nationalist crusade. Popular discourse misleadingly implies that the Paramount Chief and other traditional authorities merely adopted the political strategies fashioned by urban-based nationalists like Harry Mwaanga Nkumbula, Kenneth Kaunda and Simon Mwansa Kapwepwe, whom most writers have depicted as the true heroes of Zambia's independence.[3] Thus, we know very little about how traditional leaders at grassroots level contested imperial subjugation. Evidence suggests that once Kalonga Gawa Undi X joined the anti-colonial contest, he reconfigured some colonially-inspired institutions into a potent force with which to combat British political hegemony. Prominent among these institutions were the three Chewa Native Authorities under his control, the Eastern province Council of Chiefs and, from 1962 onward, the House of Chiefs. Ironically, these were the very institutions on which the colonial state in Northern Rhodesia relied upon to roll back the rising tide of African nationalism in the 1950s and 1960s.

But the Chewa suzerain more than just transformed colonial institutions into a means with which the subjects of empire could dismantle colonial domination. Archival accounts abundantly show that he also deployed them to enhance economic development. Such accounts indeed indicate that in the aftermath of independence, the Paramount Chief used the House of Chiefs, which outlived colonialism, to defend chiefly authority and prerogatives, to promote national integration, and, most surprisingly, to counter the politics of exclusion pursued by UNIP in its bid to

---

[3] See for example, David C. Mulford, *Zambia: The Politics of Independence, 1957-1964* (London: Oxford University Press, 1967).

monopolise power and to counter alternative political projects that posed a threat to its power. Contrary to popular discourse, then, Kalonga Gawa Undi X's role in the creation of modern Zambia transcended the politics of national liberation. Long after the Union Jack was lowered in 1964, he remained a key figure in shaping the country's social, economic, and political trajectories and hence its destiny.

This and the following chapters seek to address these themes in an effort to fill the lacunae in the historiography on Chewa sovereign. After briefly exploring shifts in his political thought and action, the present chapter examines the ways in which he transformed colonial institutions into a veritable tool of contestation for black majority rule. As a leader who employed European-authored institutions to undermine the colonial system and to advance his country's economic agenda, Kalonga Gawa Undi X stood apart from other indigenous rulers in British Africa, whom academics have caricatured as little more than agents of colonialism.[4] The next chapter will underscore the Paramount Chief's contributions in the construction of colonial and post-colonial economic destiny of Zambia. It will also illustrate the ways in which he contested UNIP's political excesses after independence.

The Genesis of Kalonga Gawa Undi X's Political Activism

The decade in which the traditional ruler assumed the Chewa chieftaincy was a politically exciting period in Central Africa as a whole and in Northern Rhodesia in particular. At the centre of the growing political excitement was the establishment in 1953 of the Federation of Rhodesia and Nyasaland by European settlers with the connivance of the British government against stiff African opposition. Africans perceived the Federation as a mere political gimmick devised by European settlers to secure a dominion status or self-government from Britain when the Federal constitution was reviewed in 1960, and in so doing, entrench their political supremacy over Africans.

In an effort to pre-empt this development, Africans rallied behind the African National Congress, a political party formed in the late 1940s. Revitalised under the leadership of Harry Nkumbula in the 1950s, the ANC, formed branches across the country and initiated a sustained campaign of

---

4 See John I. Illife, "The Age of Improvement and Differentiation," in I. N. Kimambo and A. J. Temu (eds.), *A History of Tanzania* (East African Publishing House, 1969), pp. 123-160. For a critique of this kind of scholarship, see Samuel N. Chipungu, "African Leadership under Indirect Rule in Colonial Zambia," in Samuel N. Chipungu (ed.), *Guardians in their Time: Experiences of Zambians Under Colonial Rule, 1890-1964* (London: Macmillan, 1992), pp. 50-73.

strikes, demonstrations and boycotts of white-owned businesses in order to prevail upon the British government to dissolve the Federation before its constitution came up for review in 1960. One of the strategies in this long and bitter campaign employed by the ANC and later shared by the Zambia African National Congress (the forerunner of the United National Independence Party) which broke away from the ANC in 1958, was to urge chiefs to refuse to enforce colonial laws and to encourage their subjects not to cooperate with the colonial state in its efforts to stimulate peasant commodity production after the Second World War. In so doing, the nationalist movement hoped to transform African rulers into anti-colonial elements who would subvert the authority of the colonial state, and hence bring the state to its knees.[5]

In the early 1950s, many European authorities in Eastern province all too often underplayed the growing political influence of the ANC in the area.[6] However, as more perceptive functionaries observed, the party had by that period struck a responsive chorus in most parts of the province. The Provincial Commissioner, for example, noted in his annual report of 1954 that the first two years of the Federation of Rhodesia and Nyasaland were marked by rising African preoccupation with anti-Federation politics throughout the province. The PC attributed this situation to local ANC adherents who, the official added, never ceased to vent their dislike and suspicion of the Federation even after its formal establishment.[7] By the mid-1950s, the ANC had indeed succeeded in winning several converts in the province to its gospel of nationalism. Among the converts were headmen in some chiefdoms under the Paramount Chief's jurisdiction.[8] Their growing participation in party politics expectedly raised eyebrows among European functionaries in the Eastern province. Fearing that this development would compromise efficiency in local administration, apprehensive officials began to employ "strong arm treatment" against the ANC, arresting and incarcerating its adherents.[9]

Despite the rising tempo of ANC activity within his chiefdoms and the

[5] This topic is extensively debated by Mulford, *Zambia*. See also his *The Northern Rhodesia General Election, 1962* (London: Oxford University Press, 1964) and Goodwin Mwangilwa, *Harry Mwaanga Nkumbula: A Biography of the 'Old Lion' of Zambia* (Lusaka: Multimedia Publications, 1982).

[6] Northern Rhodesia, *African Affairs Annual Report for the Year 1951*, p. 48.

[7] Northern Rhodesia, *African Affairs Annual Report for the Year 1953*, p. 62; see also Northern Rhodesia, *African Affairs Annual Report for the Year 1954*.

[8] NAZ SEC 2/708, Katete Tour Report No 2 of 1956; NAZ SEC 2/709, Katete Tour Report No. 1 of 1956

[9] See National Archives of Zambia (hereafter NAZ) SEC 2/ 694, Fort Jameson Tour Report No 11 of 1952; Northern Rhodesia, *African Affairs Annual Report for the Year 1953*, p. 62; NAZ/SEC 2/ 708, Katete Tour Report No. 2 of 1956.

participation of some of his subjects in the anti-colonial protest in the early 1950s, the first reaction of the Chewa potentate to the nationalist fervent was a mixture of indifference and hostility. In view of the active role Kalonga Gawa Undi X later played both in the freedom struggle and in cementing the national unity in independent Zambia, his early response to the nationalist struggle is enigmatic. Oral testimonies suggest that the young ruler initially perceived anti-colonial agitation, with its arm-twisting tactics of demonstrations, boycotts and strikes as a lowly affair and, therefore, demeaning to the chiefly office and status. He may have also regarded himself first and foremost as a traditional leader, whose primary responsibility was to advance the socio-economic and ritual welfare of the Chewa people, rather than that of Africans in the colony as a whole. Whatever the case, the new chief at first regarded the struggle for independence with deep scorn.[10]

By 1956, he had in fact overtly launched a verbal war against ANC leaders in the province. In a Christmas message he sent to his subordinate chiefs towards the end of that year, for instance, Kalonga Gawa Undi X castigated ANC activists in the region as "narrow and bad-minded" upstarts who "lit fire and left it to people to suffer the consequences of putting it out." He, therefore, warned his sub-chiefs and their subjects not to be swayed by what he regarded as anti-government propaganda by the ANC. He insisted that nationalist rhetoric would neither uplift people's standards of living, nor develop their country. Unsurprisingly, the Paramount Ruler repeatedly urged chiefs, whom he identified as the only legitimate rulers of the people, "to work together as one body with [the] Government of Northern Rhodesia" in finding solutions to the territory's socio-economic difficulties.[11]

The roots of the Chewa ruler's animosity to the African nationalist movement partly lay deep in the hegemonic nature of the type of nationalism that came to be associated with the top brass in the nationalist movement. From the onset of his leadership at the helm of the ANC, Harry Mwaanga Nkumbula, for one, ran the ANC autocratically. Not only did Nkumbula, as his biographer has recently noted, take unkindly to any form of criticism. He also arbitrarily dismissed his detractors within the party, supplanting them with his own loyalists.[12] Harry Mwaanga Nkumbula's

---

10 Mama Nyangu, interview cited.

11 NAZ EP1/1/36, Paramount Chief Undi's Christian Message to [Chewa] Chiefs, 28 November 1956 and Northern Rhodesia, *African Affairs Annual Report for the Year 1956*, p. 52

12 See Macola, "Harry Mwaanga Nkumbula". For a more uncritical study of Nkumbula, see

undemocratic leadership, which precipitated the breaking away of ZANC/UNIP from the ANC in 1958,[13] was apparently as abhorrent to the Chewa chief as was the party's anti-colonial rhetoric.[14] For these reasons, the traditional ruler refused to endorse the ANC and Nkumbula's leadership. He was thus not one of the 120 chiefs who in 1953 signed a petition against the Federation at his insistence of the ANC leader.[15]

Perhaps even more unacceptable to Kalonga Gawa Undi X were the arm-twisting tactics of the ANC. To his disappointment, the ANC, and later ZANC/UNIP, organised boycotts, strikes and demonstrations and perpetrated both verbal and physical violence against their political rivals in the quest for political freedom. Oral accounts indicate that even after the Paramount Chief enlisted in the anti-colonial crusade, he continued to regard these tactics as uncalled for and, perhaps, demeaning to the chiefly office and status.[16] His revulsion against the ANC's rhetoric and tactics was, moreover, reinforced by Nkumbula's unwillingness (or perhaps inability) to rein in ANC activists who poured endless epithets on anyone, including traditional rulers, who either pursued alternative political trajectories or held views that contradicted those of the party.[17]

It is in this overall context that we may appreciate the overt antipathy that the Chewa sovereign displayed against nationalist politics in the early 1950s. He perceptively saw the autocratic tendencies of the nationalist parties as something that portended a greater threat to the authority and power of the chiefly office than perhaps even colonialism itself. Unsurprisingly, he consistently implored his subordinate chiefs and subjects to cooperate wholly with colonial authorities in proscribing African nationalism. Indeed, his anti-nationalist posture earned him numerous accolades from European administrators in the province. In 1956, for insistence, the Provincial Commissioner for the Eastern province, praised Kalonga Gawa Undi X as a model illustration of the continuing wisdom, prestige and authority of an African chief.[18] But the chief's opposition to the ANC equally earned him the wrath of, and numerous death threats from the party's zealots within

---

Goodwin Mwangilwa, *Harry Nkumbula: A Biography of the 'Old Lion' of Zambia* (Lusaka: Multimedia Publications, 1982).

[13] For a recent study that downplays personalistic interpretation of the ANC-ZANC/UNIP split, see Giacomo Macola, "Harry Mwaanga Nkumula and the Formation of ZANC/UNIP: A Reinterpretation".

[14] See note 23

[15] Larmer, "History of Zambia," p. 258.

[16] Mama Nyangu, interview cited.

[17] Ibid.

[18] Northern Rhodesia, *African Affairs Annual Report for the Year 1956.*

and outside the province.[19]

The antipathy toward nationalism that the Chewa potentate exhibited in his early leadership seems to have also partly arisen from his conviction that the welfare of his people could best be advanced within the framework of colonialism. This meant utilising rather than dismantling colonial institutions. In the Christmas message cited above, he particularly singled out Western education as the "most indispensable [sic] factor", which he implored his followers "to consider" most seriously. [20] To the Chewa sovereign, modern education held the key with which his followers would unlock their creative potential and find solutions to difficulties that stood in their path to socio-economic development. Only "EDUCATED COUNTRIES," he often argued in somewhat faulty English, "make the best answers to development." Armed with modern education, the Chewa, the sovereign continued, could more creatively plan their social and economic development and thus set on to the path to elevated standards of living, civilisation and modernity. He accordingly implored Chewa subordinate

Photo 2 Paramount Chief Gawa Undi X opening a new school block in Chadiza in 1960. Courtesy of National Archives of Zambia.

---

[19] Northern Rhodesia, *African Affairs Annual Report for the Year 1958*, p. 48.
[20] NAZ EP 1/1/36, Paramount Chief Undi's Christian Message to [Chewa] Chiefs, 28 November 1956.

chiefs to cooperate closely with European authorities and missionaries in their efforts to send "as many boys and girls as possible" to school.[21]

It is obvious, then, that Kalonga Gawa Undi X's political consciousness during the early days of his reign took on an ethnic outlook. It was consequently more parochial than nationalistic. It is not by accident, therefore, that between 1953 and 1956 he reacted with glaring animosity and deepening revulsion to anti-colonial agitation. The chief distanced himself from independence politics because he regarded the nationalist agenda as both uncalled for and autocratic. As his Christian message to his subordinate chiefs implies, the suzerain feared that apart from undermining the authority and power of traditional authorities, nationalist politics would alienate the colonial state, whose cooperation and institutions he deemed as indispensable to the economic and social development of Africans. His hostility toward the African anti-colonial protest in the first half of the 1950s explains why the Chewa ruler became a darling of the provincial administrators at Fort Jameson (Chipata), earning their accolades that have already been alluded to.

It is further likely that the traditional leader's opposition to the nationalist struggle arose from his belief that political agitation was a lowly activity incommensurate with chiefly status and from the notion that his major responsibility lay with the Chewa people. This view is borne out by the fact that his early leadership was marked by his deep devotion to chiefly duties and rituals. At the time that he was combating ANC activity in the province, Kalonga Gawa Undi X, for example, undertook "extensive familiarisation tours" to all the twelve Chewa chiefdoms under his control. Wherever he went, he unfailingly urged his subordinate chiefs to cooperate with the colonial state. As these tours involved cycling over long distances, they were extremely tiring. Nonetheless, the Paramount Chief later recalled them as an immensely exciting exercise that he greatly enjoyed as a young ruler.[22]

His early career was distinguished by his conscientious dedication to traditional functions of the Chewa sovereign: settling disputes within and

---

21 NAZ EP 1/1/36, Paramount Chief Undi's Christian message to [Chewa] Chiefs, 28 November 1956; EP 1/136, Paramount Chief Undi to DC, 28 November 1956; Northern Rhodesia, *African Affairs Annual Report for the Year 1956*, p. 52. The capital letters in the quotation are in Gawa Undi's Christmas message. After independence in 1964, the Chewa ruler enthusiastically and successfully presided over a fund-raising committee tasked by the rural council in Chipata to raise £2,500 in Eastern Province for the construction of the University of Zambia. See NAZ EP 1/1/62, Minutes of the Fort Jameson Rural Council for the meeting held at Feni on 21-22 June 1965.

22 Kalonga Gawa Undi X, "Speech during the Golden Jubilee at Mkaika Palace," Katete, 3 March 2003.

between chiefdoms, selecting subordinate chiefs, performing their installation ceremonies, and carrying out other ritual obligations expected of the Chewa overlord.[23] As Chief Designate to the throne in 1952, for instance, Obister Chivunga Phiri was instrumental in the selection and installation of Kambauwa as Chief Kawaza, who later became one of the most fearless allies of the anti-colonial movement in the country.[24]

Two years after the enthronement of Chief Kawaza, Kalonga Gawa Undi X also successfully arbitrated a long-standing succession dispute involving two rival claimants to the Mbang'ombe throne: Uliya and Chilipunu. According to the District Officer-in-Charge, Katete, who attended the meeting at which the Chewa potentate resolved the wrangle, the sovereign's knowledge of the intricacies of traditional politics and local history proved as the most significant factor in the settlement of the dispute. After first summing up the arguments of the rivals, Undi X, the white administrator reported, went to "considerable trouble," invoking historical precedence in supporting Uliya's candidature. This resulted in Uliya winning the

Photo 3 Gawa Undi X installing a new subordinate chief.
Courtesy of the National Archives of Zambia.

---

[23] For the traditional duties of Kalonga Gawa Undi, see Banda, *The Chewa Kingdom*, p. 25.
[24] NAZ EP1/1/36, DC to Provincial Commissioner (PC), Fort Jameson, 18 November 1952. On Chief Kawaza's political activities, see NAZ/SEC 2/708, Katete Tour Report No 2 of 1956.

Mbango'mbe chieftainship with ninety-eight votes against Chilipunu's meagre six votes.[25] That Uliya defeated his rival with such a wide margin clearly demonstrates popular appreciation of the Paramount Chief's intervention in the succession wrangle and of his judgement. This in turn apparently endeared the Chewa Paramount Chief to his people, earning him their respect.

The Paramount Chief soon followed up his success over the Mbango'mbe succession wrangle. On 14 November 1954, he settled a potentially explosive central quarrel between Chiefs Mwangala and Zingalume.[26] Kalonga Gawa Undi X, whose knowledge of the boundaries of Chewa chiefdoms seems to have been widely acclaimed among chiefs and European officials alike, resolved the dispute by elucidating the historical origins of the two chiefdoms and their boundaries. Diplomatically, he argued that the boundary dispute between the concerned parties was as unnecessary as it was retrogressive because the rivals were brothers who shared a common ancestry. Again invoking historical precedence, colonial reports note that the overlord illuminated the demarcations between the rival chiefdoms so fairly that European officials in the province felt that the land dispute between the rival chiefs would not resurface in future.[27]

It may be surmised from the suzerain's initial hostility to the anti-colonial protest and his dedication to chiefly responsibilities that Kalonga Gawa Undi X was at first more concerned with preserving the status quo. Yet in 1957, barely three years after assuming the Chewa throne, the Paramount Chief enlisted in the nationalist crusade by joining Harry Mwaanga Nkumbula's political party. He henceforth became an ardent opponent against colonial rule, and when Kenneth Kaunda and other more radical leaders left the ANC in 1958 due to Nkumbula's dictatorial tendencies, the Chief joined hands with Kaunda. The radical shift in his perception of colonialism was no less the consequence of the studies that Kalonga Gawa Undi X underwent in Britain in 1956-1957 than the result of the rising popular political militancy in Chewa chiefdoms that confronted the traditional ruler upon his return from overseas in the latter year. The growing political militancy in the chiefdoms issued from the spread of the nationalist struggle from urban areas, where it had long been largely confined, to

25 NAZ EP 1/1/12, District Officer-in-Charge, Katete, to DC, 6 November 1954.
26 NAZ EP 1/1/12, Minutes of the meeting held to resolve land troubles between Chief Mwangala and Chief Zingalume held at Kamphinga Village, Chief Zingalume, 14 November 1954.
27 NAZ EP 1/1/12, Minutes of the meeting held to resolve land troubles between Chief Mwangala and Chief Zingalume, Zingalume, 14 November 1954

virtually all areas in the colony as the nationalist leaders mobilised mass support to exert more pressure upon European settlers now more than determined to hold on to political power.[28]

This unprecedented development was as much fuelled by the political concessions that Roy Welensky wrested from the British government in 1957 as it was fuelled by the Federal Amendment and Federal Assembly Acts that the settler-dominated Federal government passed during the same period to frustrate African political advancement.[29] Similarly, rising rural political agitation was lubricated by the "expectations of independence" enlivened by the glowing promises (still unfulfilled today) that nationalist leaders and activists in rural areas made to their supporters to sustain the momentum of the freedom struggle.[30] Consequently, by 1957 when the chief returned to Eastern province from Europe, nationalism had engulfed even the remotest parts of his chiefdoms.[31]

It is within the context of the growing politicisation of his chiefdoms in the late 1950s that we may perhaps best appreciate why Kalonga Gawa Undi X embraced the nationalist movement after his return from Britain. With the rising political temperature in areas under his jurisdiction, which sometimes erupted in fatal clashes between ZANC and ANC activists, his earlier hostility to the nationalist struggle was no longer tenable. Undoubtedly, remaining hostile or indifferent to the nationalist struggle would have cost him the support, respect and the loyalty of the rising number of his followers who converted to nationalism in the late 1950s. As a perceptive European official noted in 1957, Kalonga Gawa Undi X, could ill-afford to alienate the support of this expanding number of followers by remaining indifferent to or maintaining an antagonistic stance towards the politics of decolonisation. Thus, at the risk of vexing the colonial administration or even inviting dethronement, the chief, in the colonial officer's terms, began to play to the public gallery.[32]

Crucial as internal dynamics were to influencing the Paramount Chief's attitude towards colonial rule and African nationalism, it cannot be disputed that his studies in Britain, under which he attended a govern-

---

[28] See Cherry Gertzel and Morris Szeftel, "Politics in an Africa urban setting: the role of the Copperbelt in the transition to the one-party state," in Cheery Gertzel, Carolyn Baylies and Morris Szeftel (eds.), *The Dynamics of the One Party State in Zambia* (Manchester: Manchester University Press, 1984), pp. 118-162

[29] For details on this topic, see Mulford, *Zambia*, pp.51-52

[30] See Macola, G. "'It Means as if we are Excluded from the Good Freedom': Thwarted Expectations of Independence in the Luapula Province of Zambia," *Journal of African History* 47 (2006), pp. 43-56.

[31] Joseph Galeta Mbewe, interview cited.

[32] Northern Rhodesia, *African Affairs Annual Report for the Year 1957*.

ment-sponsored course in local government administration at the South Devon College, Torquay, in 1956,[33] also played key role in influencing the traditional ruler's political consciousness. The course at Torquay placed a great deal of emphasis on the democratic principles of the local government system in Britain. This seems to have brought in sharp focus in the mind of the young chief the despotic nature of British rule in Northern Rhodesia, where European officials dominated Africans, used their monopoly of power to impose or depose chiefs, and, most ominously, denied imperial subjects a voice in law-making organs, including the Legislative and Executive Councils. This realisation later underscored the potentate's efforts to reform the Native Authorities he controlled in Eastern province so that they became, as we shall see, a no minor force against colonial subjugation.

But while still in the UK, the traditional ruler's most significant education apparently issued from outside lecture halls. The absence of organised racism in Britain and mainland Europe meant that Kalonga Gawa Undi X experienced no institutionalised racial discrimination in Europe, where, while en route to Northern Rhodesia at the end of 1957, he also visited Rome and the Vatican.[34] The Paramount Chief was particularly struck by the fact that blacks in Europe were permitted to eat in restaurants, sleep in hostels shared by whites, and visit any place patronised by white people. Perhaps to his own surprise, Kalonga Gawa Undi X himself was invited to spend his Christmas vacation between 21st December 1956 and 14th January 1957 with White Fathers in Heston, Middlesex, and later with Father J. P. Moran (on leave from Chipata) and his family in Murray, Ireland. He attended a garden party at Buckingham Palace with the reigning Queen of England.[35] These experiences must have left profound impact on the Chief from colonial Zambia, where indigenous people were excluded from "European Only" spaces, denied individual and civil liberties, and treated as second class citizens in the land of their own birth.[36]

But perhaps even more significant to shaping the Chewa ruler's political consciousness than the informal education the ruler encountered in Europe were the social connections he cultivated with people he met there from various other parts of the British Empire. Most of such acquaintances,

---

[33] NAZ EP1/1/36, Kuunika [Newsletter] No. 3 of 1956; Northern Rhodesia, *African Affairs Annual Report for the Year 1956*, p. 51.

[34] Gawa Undi X, "Speech".

[35] Gawa Undi X, "Speech" and NAZ EP 1/136, Kuunika No. 3 of 1957.

[36] These experiences were shared by other blacks who visited Europe in the 1950s and 1960s. See for example, Andrew J. DeRoche, *Andrew Young: Civil Rights Ambassador* (Washington, DC: SR Books, 2003), pp. 7-8.

Kalonga Gawa Undi X would recall many years later, were united in their antipathy against British colonial domination and hegemony. Their abhorrence against colonialism seems to have particularly come in sharp relief in 1957 in Cardiff, South Wales, where the Paramount Chief met on a course sponsored by the British Council thirty-four other students from fifteen British colonies and ex-colonies. Among his new acquaintances were chiefs, who, to the surprise of the Northern Rhodesian Chief, were vehemently opposed to imperial domination on the colonial periphery, and they articulated sophisticated economic and political ideas.[37] To the surprise of the Chewa traditional ruler, they also demanded for the immediate dissolution of the British Empire and strongly opposed the Federation of Rhodesia and Nyasaland in Central Africa. Some of his classmates indeed often openly wondered why Africans in the region had not yet taken up arms to drive out their white tormentors who had engineered the Federation of Rhodesia and Nyasaland.

Ironically, one of the most outspoken critics of the Federation who apparently left the most lasting impression on Kalonga Gawa Undi X was Maurice Katowa, a fellow chief from Northern Rhodesia. A former teacher, Katowa was installed after the Second World War as Chief Mapanza of the Tonga people of Choma in Zambia's Southern province. Mapanza Maurice Katowa surprised the colonial administration when he joined the ANC and became an indomitable opponent of the Federation in the early 1950s. In retrospect, his involvement in ANC activity may be construed as a double-edged tactical manoeuvre. Through his active participation in ANC politics, he sought to lend his chiefly influence to the liberation movement. On the other hand, Chief Mapanza certainly intended to use political activism to attenuate ANC opposition to post-war government-inspired economic agenda that the Tonga ruler perceived as beneficial to his own people but which the nationalist party and later the United National Independence Party strongly opposed as part of their anti-colonial crusade.

By the time Maurice Katowa joined the Chewa Chief at Torquay in the latter part of 1957, the former had since become the Branch Secretary of the ANC in Choma, notwithstanding constant threats of dethronement from the colonial government. Chief Mapanza's political activism combined with his ambitious development agenda had by that time yielded impressive results in the form of modern social conveniences like health care centres and schools built near his palace. By the early 1960s, Mapanza

---

[37] NAZ EP 1/1/36, Kuunika, No 3 of 1957, 1 March 1957.

presided over one of the wealthiest chiefdoms in the whole territory.[38] His successes as chief, politician, and agent of modernity coupled with the colonial government's failure to depose him for his political activities apparently removed whatever lingering doubts Kalonga Gawa Undi X may still have harboured with regard to what role chiefs could play in the struggle for freedom. Unsurprisingly, the Chewa ruler maintained very close ties with Chief Mapanza after they both returned to Northern Rhodesia.

Back in the colony, towards the end of 1950s, the two traditional leaders worked hand in hand in forcefully demanding for the abolition of the Federation and in championing rural economic development. Both rulers, as shown later, also participated as representatives of the territory's chiefs in the constitutional talks held in Lusaka in October 1960 and, later that year, at Lancaster House, London. Moreover, between 1962 and 1972 Chiefs Mapanza and Gawa Undi X served as perhaps the most influential members of the Standing Committee of the House Chiefs, respectively presiding with unrivalled records over the House as its first and third Chairmen.[39]

The significance of the social contacts and of the formal and informal education Kalonga Gawa Undi X underwent in Europe to shaping his political consciousness cannot be over-emphasised. Soon after the arrival of the Paramount Chief from England in late 1957, an admiring white administrative functionary who met the suzerain at Fort Jameson (now Chipata) observed that Gawa Undi X returned with a "much wider [political and economic] outlook". The official attributed this situation to the Paramount Chief's "overseas education".[40] This observation was soon confirmed. Before the year ended, the Chewa traditional ruler, like Chief Mapazanza Maurice Katowa before him, "strayed into the field [of nationalist] politics" by joining the ANC, much to the discontent of European administrators in the province.[41] Henceforth, the Chewa potentate increasingly turned into a bitter enemy of the Federation of Rhodesia and Nyasaland and of white settler political aspirations. He also, much to the bewilderment of colonial officials in the province who earlier saw him as a malleable ally in proscribing nationalism, became one of the leading figures in the nationalist move-

---

[38] See Samuel N. Chipungu, *The State, Technology and Peasant Differentiation in Zambia: A Case Study of the Southern Province* (Lusaka: Historical Association of Zambia, 1988), Chapter V.

[39] NAZ EP 1/1/54, Clerk of the House of Chiefs to PC, Eastern Province, 8 January 1963.

[40] Northern Rhodesia, *African Affairs Annual Report for the Year 1957*, p. 55.

[41] Northern Rhodesia, *African Affairs Annual Report for the Year 1958*, p. 50.

ment. Well up to 1964, Kalonga Gawa Undi X forcefully indicted the ideology and practice of colonialism, fearlessly demanding the immediate destruction of the Central African Federation and the transfer of power to the black majority.

To accurately assess what influence the "wider outlook" and involvement of the Paramount Chief in nationalist politics exerted on the independence struggle in colonial Zambia, it is first essential to unravel, however briefly, the wider political context in which he became embroiled in the bubbling anti-colonial cauldron. The political situation that Kalonga Gawa Undi X encountered on his return from Britain was dramatically changing, with constitutional issues looming extremely large at both territorial and Federal levels. Territorially, European settlers, threatened by the rising storm of African nationalism, were now deeply dissatisfied with the 1953 constitutional arrangements, which denied them outright majorities in both the Legislative and Executive Councils. Under these arrangements, the settlers had successfully pressurised the British Government to permit them retain a franchise that effectively excluded the majority of Africans from the governing process since the 1920s. They had also secured Britain's approval of their demand to raise the number of elected un-officials who represented white settlers in the Legislative Council to twelve out of the twenty-six members in the Council.

However, this still denied them the clear majority they wanted. This is because the 1953 constitution also provided for eight elected officials, two nominated Europeans who represented African interests, and four Africans appointed by the Governor from the African Representative Council. Moreover, although the constitution reduced the officials' majority in the Executive Council by one seat, one of the four elected un-officials admitted to that Council in the 1950s was nominated to represent African interests there.[42] Disappointed with this constitutional arrangement and worried by the rising tide of African political agitation, Europeans in Northern Rhodesia renewed their pre-Federation demand for self-government from Britain.

But their quest for self-determination in Northern Rhodesia fell on deaf ears in Britain. Thus, as a leading analyst of the politics of decolonisation in Zambia perceptively remarks, the initiative for European constitutional progress in the territory from the mid-1950s passed on to the Federal Government in Salisbury (Harare), now under the control of Roy

---

42 Mulford, *Zambia*, pp. 48-61. For a more recent study of issues raised here, see Bizeck Jube Phiri, *A Political History of Zambia: From the Colonial Period to the 3rd Republic, 1890-2001* (Trenton NJ and Asmara, Africa World Press, Inc., 2004).

Welensky.[43] Welensky, who had earlier began his political career in Northern Rhodesia and became the Federal Prime Minister in 1956, was a relentless nemesis of African political advancement. Politically adept, he managed in August 1957 to wrest from a reluctant British Government some major concessions for the Federation of Rhodesia and Nyasaland. Under these concessions, which extremely alarmed Africans, the British Government conferred on the Federal Government more responsibility over external affairs, abandoned its right to legislate for the Federation as earlier provided for in the Federal legislation, and allowed European civil servants to settle in any part of the Federal area upon retirement. Most alarming to Africans, Britain further endorsed at least in principle the Prime Minister's proposal for the expansion of the Federal Assembly, his demand to abolish the right of Federal member states to either secede from or amalgamate against the Federation, and, finally, his demand to accelerate the settlers' journey toward the achievement of self-rule from Britain when the Federal Review took place in 1960.[44]

Britain's endorsement of these constitutional proposals not merely dismayed Africans in Northern Rhodesia. It also convinced them that the British Government was now more than ever willing to sell them down the cold river of white supremacy. Their alarm was not reduced when Welensky, now emboldened by Britain's positive attitude toward settler aspirations, followed up his political successes by introducing in September 1957 the highly controversial Federal Constitution Amendment Bill and the Federal Franchise Bill. These bills were designed to enlarge European representation in the Federal Assembly, while simultaneously reducing the African voice in the Assembly.[45] African apprehension grew even more precipitously when Sir Arthur Benson, the Governor of Northern Rhodesia, issued an equally controversial White Paper a year later, ostensibly intended to foster racial partnership between Africans and European settlers. But, as African nationalists feared, the implementation of the White Paper with its resultant constitution would have conferred a very narrow franchise on the emerging but still tiny class of educated Africans, further disenfranchising the majority of Africans.[46]

In Northern Rhodesia, African response to these political manoeuvres

---

[43] Mulford, *Zambia*, p. 49.
[44] Ibid., pp. 51-52.
[45] Ibid., pp. 51-52.
[46] Ibid, pp. 56-106. See also Peter Calvocoressi, *World Politics since 1945*, sixth Edition (London and New York: 1991, [1968]) p. 560.

by European settlers and the British government was swift. The more militant members of the African National Congress led by Kenneth Kaunda, Simon Kapwepwe and Munukaumbwa Sipalo roundly denounced Roy Welensky and the British government's political machinations as vehemently as they rejected Sir Arthur Benson's White Paper with its proposed constitution. When Harry Nkumbula seemed to countenance the controversial constitution with its so-called politics of racial partnership in 1958, the militants broke ranks with the ANC to form the Zambia African National Congress (the forerunner of the United National Independence Party, UNIP). From the outset mounted, ZANC/UNIP waged a bitter and sometimes violent campaign against the Federal government. Predictably, the new party persistently called for the secession of Northern Rhodesia from the Federation, for outright African majorities in the Legislative and Executive Councils, and for the destruction of the Federation before 1960.

Colonial Institutions and the Contest for Political Power

The political euphoria marked by mounting white settler drive for political ascendancy and growing African determination to break that supremacy and attain self-government marked the context in which the protagonist enlisted in the nationalist combat for independence in the late 1950s. He was now convinced that the political aspirations of Europeans in Central Africa were not only racialist and pathetically undemocratic but also irrevocably at variance with those of Africans. To Kalonga Gawa Undi X, the constitutional machinations of the Federal, British and Northern Rhodesian governments amounted to little more than tricks by which European settlers wanted to entrench their racial and political supremacy, to expand their wealth, and to suppress African aspirations at the minimal cost of granting a limited franchise to the emerging African middle class in the region. As a corollary, Kalonga Gawa Undi X allied himself with the nationalist movement determined to liberate the country from foreign domination. The course that the colonial state had sponsored the Paramount Chief to attend at Torquay in England came to haunt it.

The engagement of the traditional leader with the politics of liberation coincided with the colonial state's growing determination to crush the nationalist crusade. To do so, European authorities began to recruit state-controlled institutions in its counter-nationalist strategy. In rural areas, this meant converting Native Authorities and Native Courts, through which the authorities collected taxes and maintained law and order since the

46

1930s, into an instrument for proscribing nationalism.[47] The state hoped to turn Native Authorities and chiefs into its anti-nationalist allies in two main ways. First, it persistently implored them to enact orders under which they could ban nationalists from areas under their sway and suppress any political activities they deemed unlawful. Native Authorities together with their courts were thus increasingly pressed to arrest, to prosecute and to imprison ANC and UNIP "agitators." Second, the colonial government dismissed or threatened to dismiss Native Authority personnel and chiefs with pro-nationalist sympathies.[48]

To fill the vacuum created by dismissals, the government began to appoint to the Native Authority system traditional rulers and councillors not on the basis of their royal connections in line with the tenets of Indirect Rule but rather on the strength of their academic qualifications, or, more accurately, their subservience to the colonial state. In either case, this was a clear violation of the system of Indirect Rule that at least theoretically placed a premium upon royal affinity in the recruitment of Native Authority staff.[49] The policy to staff the Native Authority system with pro-government sympathisers sometimes unavoidably led to the appointment of chiefs whose royal ties were at best tenuous and at worst non-existent.

Some chiefs gave in to this official blackmail. For instancem, in a move that immensely elated the Provincial Commissioner for the Eastern Province, M.G. Billing, Chief Mbangombe of Katete banned ANC leaders from holding meetings in his chiefdom in 1957; so did several other chiefs elsewhere in the province.[50] But Gawa Undi X succumbed to neither official blackmail nor intimidation. For between 1957 and 1958, he openly supported the ANC and, after the party split up in the latter year, switched his allegiance to ZANC/UNIP. His nascent opposition to white misrule manifested itself in his ironic, double-edged agenda. On the one hand, the Chief endeavoured to strengthen the edifice of the Native Authorities under his own sway. Gawa Undi X, on the other hand, deployed these institutions to

[47] For a detailed discussion on the creation of Native Authorities in colonial Zambia, see Kusum Datta, 'The Policy of Indirect Rule in Northern Rhodesia (Zambia), 1924-1953, (unpublished doctoral thesis, University of London, 1976).

[48] See Samuel N. Chipungu, "African Leaders under Indirect Rule in Colonial Zambia," in Samuel N. Chipungu (ed.), *Guardians in their Time: Experiences of Zambians under Colonial Rule, 1890-1964* (London: Macmillan, 1992), pp. 50-73.

[49] NAZ SEC 2/709, Comments by Provincial Commissioner on Katete Tour Report No 1 of 1956. See also Chipungu, "African Leadership," pp. 53-54. For detailed studies on Indirect Rule in Northern Rhodesia, see Datta, "Policy of Indirect Rule in Zambia," Ben Kakoma, 'Colonial Administration in Northern Rhodesia: A Case Study of Administration in Mwinilunga District, 1900-1939,' (unpublished master's thesis, University of Auckland, 1977).

[50] NAZ SEC 2/707, Comments by PC on Katete Tour Report No 4 of 1957.

weaken the colonial state itself, and, as demonstrated in the next chapter, to foster the welfare of his own people.

The Chewa Paramount Chief perceived the colonial state's drive to fill Native Authorities with pro-government chiefs and personnel as a deliberate move by which the state could frustrate African political aspirations. To emasculate this policy, Kalonga Gawa Undi X took advantage of the law that permitted paramount chiefs in the territory to nominate appointees to Native Authorities, in keeping with the tenets of Indirect Rule. He began to insist on royalty as the prime criterion for employing chiefs, clerks, court assessors, messengers (kapasos) and councillors who headed various departments (education, health, agriculture, etc) in the Supreme Chewa Native Authority headquartered at his Nyaviombo palace at Chiparamba, Chipata, and in the sub-Native Authorities at Kagoro and Chipili in Katete.

In retrospect, the insistence by the potentate on appointing royals to the local Native Authority system should be thought of as a calculated strategy. Through this strategy, he firstly aimed at undercutting European administrators' intention to fill Chewa Native Authorities with stooges. Secondly, by insisting on royalty as the most important qualification for employment in his Native Authorities, the traditional ruler hoped to carve enough space for himself to appoint staff and chiefs who had converted to the nationalist ideology. In this way, he succeeded in filling most of the vacancies in the local administrative structures under his control with personnel committed to suppressing British colonial rule. As a sequel, chiefs and headmen who supported the liberation struggle became the most conspicuous figures in all three Chewa Native Authorities, a point that European administrators in the province conceded in the late 1950s.[51] As the administrators were fully aware, it was these men who provided the backbone of the nationalist leadership at grassroots level in most parts of the Chewa nation in the late 1950s and early 1960s.[52] It is paradoxical, then, that colonial functionaries in the province expected such employees to be the vanguard against the spread of ANC and UNIP "subversive propaganda".

Kalonga Gawa Undi X did not stop short of infusing his Native Authorities with converts to the gospel of nationalism. He also successfully lobbied for the discontinuation of the long-established practice under which

---

[51] NAZ SEC 2/707, Comments by PC on Katete Tour Report No 4 of 1957; see also NAZ SEC 2/711, Katete Tour Report No. 10 of 1958. On the same file see, Katete Tour Report, J. E. Madocks, District Commissioner to Provincial Commissioner, 17 December 1958

[52] Northern Rhodesia, *African Affairs Annual Report for the Year 1958*, p. 50; see also, NAZ SEC 2/710, Katete Tour Report No. 12 of 1957.

the colonial state paid Native Authority staff, including chiefs, half of their subsidies, while the Supreme Chewa Native Authority at Nyaviombo paid them the remainder. As the Supreme Authority became more prosperous from the late 1950s, the Paramount Chief supplanted this practice with a scheme through which all the Native Authority employees' emoluments were wholly paid by the Supreme Authority itself.[53] The implications of this fiscal reform were far-reaching. In addition to securing a measure of fiscal autonomy from the state for the Chewa Native Authorities, the reform largely neutralised European officials' tendency to withhold subsidies from Native Authority personnel and chiefs whom they saw as either inefficient or as ANC or UNIP activists. This inevitably subverted the functionaries' propensity to use monetary blandishments to dictate the political ideology and praxis of those who worked within the Native Authority system under the Paramount Chief.

In the latter part of the 1950s, he equally thwarted a decentralisation scheme designed by white officials in the province to devolve to the sub-Native Authorities at Chipili and Kagoro executive and fiscal powers hitherto monopolised by the Supreme Chewa Native Authority at Chiparamba, over which the Chewa overlord personally presided.[54] The rationale behind this proposed scheme, white officials in Chipata argued, was to enhance the administrative efficiency of the two sub-Authorities. But had the scheme been implemented, it would have also drastically reduced the authority of the Supreme Native Authority, consequently eroding the power, prestige and the influence of the Paramount Chief.[55] Through successfully defending the executive and financial powers vested in the Supreme Native Authority at his headquarters, Kalonga Gawa Undi X ensured that the sub-Native Authorities at Kagoro and Chipili fell in line with his desire to give constitutional issues top billing in their agenda. It is little wonder, therefore, that although he seldom presided over sub Native Authority meetings at Chipili and Kagoro due to his onerous political and chiefly commitments, both Authorities kept the anti-colonial flame burning throughout the 1950s and the 1960s. Their meetings, like those of the Supreme Authority at Nyaviombo, provided an occasion for intense opposition to the Federation, to the Benson constitution and to the Monckton Commission appointed in the latter period by the British Government to gather African opinion on the Federal constitution. Both Authorities also

---

53 Northern Rhodesia, *African Affairs Annual Report for the Year 1958*, p. 50.
54 Ibid.
55 Ibid.

took an active part in planning demonstrations, boycotts and strikes against colonial rule and in raising funds for the liberation movement.[56]

Kalonga Gawa Undi X Obister Chivunga Phiri's reforms or objections to state-inspired reforms may at face value appear to have been cosmetic. However, through stocking the local Native Authorities with pro-nationalists and by winning for them some measure of fiscal independence from the colonial state, the Paramount Chief strengthened the fabric of the Chewa Native Authority system in the crusade to obliterate foreign oppression and subjugation. These reforms enabled him to transform the Authorities he controlled into a veritable instrument of anti-colonial protest. Unsurprisingly, his reforms soon placed him on a collision path with colonial agents. This collision was inevitable, for the Paramount Chief's reforms together with his open support for nationalism confounded British authorities' efforts to reduce the functions of Native Authorities to the maintenance of law and order, collection of taxes, and proscription of the African nationalist struggle for freedom after the Second World War.[57]

The extent to which the traditional leader succeeded in strengthening the hand of Chewa Native Authority system in the battle against British hegemony is not too difficult to gauge. Successive generations of European officials in the province between the 1950s and 1960s frequently complained that Native Authority meetings at Chipili, Nyaviombo and Kagoro always amounted to bitter opposition to territorial and federal constitutional proposals, incessant verbal abuse against state functionaries who upheld colonialism, and above all, unceasing campaign for the dissolution of the Federation and for black majority rule.[58] These officers also often lamented that the Native Authorities under Kalonga Gawa Undi X regarded themselves "as in competition with, rather than as a part of the central administrative machine".[59]

Clearly, then, Paramount Chief Kalonga Gawa Undi X transformed Chewa Native Authorities into a vehicle of the destruction of colonial power and of the construction of counter-hegemonic black power. He therefore distanced himself and his subordinate chiefs from the colonial government's agenda to suppress African nationalist aspirations. It is para-

---

[56] See NAZ SEC 2/710, Katete Tour Report No. 12 of 1957.

[57] For details on the colonial Government's drive to restrict the functions of Native Authorities to these roles in the 1950, see Chipungu, "African Leadership"; Samuel N. Chipungu, "Accumulation from within: the Boma Class and the Native Treasury in colonial Zambia," in Chipungu (ed.), *Guardians in their Time*, pp. 74-96.

[58] Northern Rhodesia, *African Affairs Annual Report for the Year 1957*, p. 48.

[59] Northern Rhodesia, *African Affairs Annual Report for the Year 1958*, p. 50.

doxical that the ruler prosecuted his nationalist activity through state-engi-
neered institutions. This paradox is all the more remarkable as European
authorities hoped to mobilise African chiefs and state institutions throughout the colony to abate the suffocating wind of the African nationalism. The
Chewa Paramount Chief's unbending commitment to the nationalist crusade indeed earned him endless threats of deportation from European
officials both in the province and in Lusaka from the late 1950s onward.[60]

The significance of Kalonga Gawa Undi X Obister Chivunga Phiri's
involvement in nationalist politics went beyond reconfiguring Native Authorities into an arm of contestation for majority rule. Once the traditional
leader enlisted in the independence struggle, he also evidently made effective use of the vast network of personal, social and political relations he had
earlier cultivated to attract to the nationalist fold more and more political
converts.[61] Oral accounts suggest that in the late 1950s and 1960s, Gawa
Undi X persuaded many commoners, headmen and chiefs within and
outside Chewa areas to join in the struggle for independence. Among these
were Chiefs Mwangala and Zingalume, whose boundary dispute Gawa
Undi X had earlier resolved. Others included members of the royal family:
cousins, nieces and nephews, etc.[62]

Some of these new converts seem to have been initially opposed to the
freedom campaign, but they were eventually drawn into the nationalist
fold due to the Paramount Chief's influence. The total effect of all this was
that the Chewa overlord with other traditional leaders in the province
effectively embedded and articulated the liberation discourse within the
framework of prevailing personal, social and political relations. This inevitably eased local assimilation of the nationalist agenda. From the late 1950s
onward, this went a long way in capturing popular political imagination
and support for the United National Independence Party. As a corollary,
chiefdoms under the traditional ruler became a bastion of UNIP. A colonial
official admitted as much in 1958 when he remarked that anti-colonial
protests reached even the remotest villages in Chewa chiefdoms. In these
chiefdoms, according to the state official, constitutional debates out-
weighed all other concerns among the majority of the local people.[63]

---

[60] Kalonga Gawa Undi X, "Speech".

[61] For an excellent analysis of the value of personal networks in mobilising mass political support
for UNIP in an urban setting both before and after Independence, see Peter Harries-Jones,
Freedom and Labour: Mobilization and Political Control on the Zambian Copperbelt (Oxford: Basil
Blackwell, 1975).

[62] Informal interview with Edward Nyirongo, Undi's grandson, Mkaika, 13 November 2005.

[63] Northern Rhodesia, *African Affairs Annual Report for the Year 1958*, p. 48.

From this perspective, it is safe to assert that the significance of Kalonga Gawa Undi X to the nationalist movement rested less on his involvement in constitutional talks than on his ability to win mass support for the liberation movement. His ability to articulate the nationalist cause in local terms and to embed it within existing social relations meant that he familiarised the nationalist discourse so that it came to make cultural sense to his followers. A respected ruler, he also bestowed on the independence movement a degree of credibility and respectability that captured local imagination perhaps much more than urban-based "agitators" like Harry Nkumbula and Kenneth Kaunda could ever hope to accomplish. This view is all the more convincing given the ephemeral nature of their political activities in the countryside, coupled with their inability to articulate the nationalist cause in local languages.

Conversant with Chewa political rhetoric, intrigue and idioms, the Paramount Chie was better placed to articulate and popularise the nationalist cause through familiar or familiarised grammar. In this vein, he was able to explain with greater clarity and persuasion why, for example, white settler's constitutional proposals were unacceptable, why UNIP split from the ANC in 1958, and why it was important to do away with alien rule, to support the freedom struggle, and to pay subscription fees to the liberation movement. Such clarity was rewarded. From 1959, UNIP quickly won popular support in Chewa-speaking areas, and the Chief's efforts to raise funds for the party proved a resounding success. In the latter part of the 1950s, Gawa Undi X successfully appealed to his subjects for funds to enable him to go to England to explain to the British government why Africans in Northern Rhodesia were opposed to the Federal constitution. So generous were their contributions that by the time the Paramount Chief left for England in 1958, he had sufficient funds for a return airfare, upkeep and accommodation in Britain.[64]

The traditional ruler met no success in England, for the British government made no significant changes to the Federal constitution, paying no attention to African demand for the destruction of the Federation of Rhodesia and Nyasaland. Apparently, Kalonga Gawa Undi X remained undeterred. Back in Northern Rhodesia, he renewed with vigour the anti-Federation campaign and demand for the immediate transfer of political power to Africans. As part of this campaign, the Chief, now one of the linchpins in Kenneth Kaunda's United National Independence Party with

---

[64] Gawa Undi X, "Speech".

its non-racialist policy, took an unwavering stand against the Monckton Commission appointed in 1960 by the British government to gather public opinion in Northern Rhodesia and Nyasaland *vis-à-vis* the future of the Federation of Rhodesia and Nyasaland. Since the Commission's terms of reference omitted the question of the secession of Northern Rhodesia from the Federation and of its dissolution, Kalonga Gawa Undi X saw the Monckton Commission as yet another British trick to prolong the future of the much-despised Federation.[65] He therefore backed UNIP's countrywide campaign of demonstrations, strikes and boycott of the Commission. In a spirited attempt to champion the campaign, the sovereign personally travelled the length and breadth of the Eastern province, urging Chewa and non-Chewa chiefs alike not to testify before the Commission.

That this campaign was a success is beyond doubt. Throughout the chiefdoms under his jurisdiction, neither individuals nor any of the three Chewa Native Authorities appeared before the Monckton Commission.[66] Within the province as a whole, only Native Authorities in Lundazi and in Chipata dominated by ANC supporters appeared before the Commission in accordance with their party's directive not to boycott it. Ultimately, it was this decision coupled with the Chewa Chief's uncompromising stand toward the Monckton Commission that marked the demise of the ANC in nearly all Chewa-speaking areas, as indeed in most other parts of the province. As a sequel, the party lost a huge following to UNIP, a misfortune from which ANC never recovered until it was legislated into extinction with the abolition of the multi-party system of governance in Zambia in 1973.[67]

As the 1960s drew to a close, Kalonga Gawa Undi X seems to have explicitly recognised the need to broaden the battle for political freedom far beyond the confines of Chewa Native Authorities and the province in order to turn up the heat of the struggle. To this end, in the 1960s onward he increasingly cooperated with other chiefs in the territory's Council of Chiefs renowned for their anti-colonial stand. The Paramount Chief began to collaborate particularly with Chiefs Chikwanda of the Bisa-Bemba in Mpika, Ikelenge of the Lunda in Mwinilunga, and, least surprisingly, Chief

---

[65] Northern Rhodesia, *African Affairs Annual Report for the Year 1960*, p. 51 and Mulford, *Zambia*, p. 148.

[66] Northern Rhodesia, *African Affairs Annual Report for the Year 1960*.

[67] On the failure of the Movement for Multi-Party Democracy to break UNIP hold on the Eastern Province in more recent years, see Jan Kees Van Donge, "Zambia, Kaunda and Chiluba: Enduring Patterns of Political Culture," in John A. Wiseman, *Democracy and Political Change in Sub-Saharan Africa* (London and New York: Rutledge, 1995), p. 193.

Mapanza of the Tonga in Choma. Together with Kalonga Gawa Undi X, these chiefs represented fellow traditional rulers in the Council, and all of them shared deep abhorrence against the Federation and colonialism.

Collectively, the four traditional authorities were instrumental in turning the territorial Council of Chiefs into a mouthpiece of the liberation movement, notwithstanding British authorities' overt intention to recruit the Council against African nationalism. The chiefs' eagerness to articulate anti-colonial sentiments through this institution most vividly surfaced in October 1960, when white authorities in Lusaka invited the Council to deliberate their proposals on constitutional reforms pending the Lancaster House Constitutional Conference scheduled to commence later in the year. Although the traditional rulers' franchise proposals somewhat diverged from UNIP's quest for an outright universal suffrage, most of their other demands came as a rude shock to the colonial government in their similarity to those of nationalist leaders.

Like UNIP officials, Chiefs Kalonga Gawa Undi X, Ikelenge, Mapanza and Chikwanda demanded for black majorities in the Legislative and Executive Councils, for severing the colony's ties with the Federation, and for holding the territory's constitutional conference before the Federal Constitutional Review at the end of the year.[68] They also successfully lobbied for the establishment of a House of Chiefs through which they would consider bills from the Legislative Council and forward to the colony's governor their recommendations on questions of public interest.[69] Made under intense opposition from colonial authorities, these proposals predictably elated Kenneth Kaunda, the UNIP President. "It is all so wonderful," enthused the visibly jubilant party President in a letter to a leading Chewa nationalist. "I pray," Kaunda continued, "that no amount of pressure will be too strong for them to resist. They have made a very good move and I am sure that they will not be disappointed when we take over".[70]

UNIP thus recognised the importance of the constitutional proposals that chiefs in the Council of Chiefs advanced. In so doing, the party acknowledged its indebtedness to the four chiefs who had stirred the Council towards sharing a common political platform with the liberation movement. But the appreciation of the valuable contribution of these chiefs did not stop at the doors of UNIP and the ANC alone. In December 1960,

---

68 Mulford, *Zambia*, p. 169.
69 For details on the role of the House of Chiefs see, NAZ EP 1/1/54, Cabinet Office Circular No. 39 of 1964
70 The quotation is cited in Mulford, *Zambia*, p. 170.

twenty-five members comprising the electoral college of the territorial Council of Chiefs itself elected the four rulers as their delegates to the Lancaster constitutional conference in London. This demonstrated the high esteem, trust, and respect which Kalonga Gawa Undi X Obister Chivunga Phiri and his three colleagues commanded among other traditional rulers across the country.

In London, the chiefs' delegates, ANC and UNIP again spoke with one voice in backing the proposals advanced earlier in Lusaka. While there, the chiefs came full circle with UNIP's demand for an electoral system enshrined in the principle of universal suffrage.[71] But not all their demands were accepted by the British Government or by the representatives of white settlers at the talks. However, the fact that their proposals echoed those of the ANC and UNIP was sufficient to persuade the British government that the liberation movement in colonial Zambia had mustered the sufficient cohesion, unity and power that the British had always regarded as a prerequisite to the granting of political independence to protectorates on the imperial frontier.[72] Moreover, even though some of the traditional leaders' demands in London were not accepted by the British Government, they nonetheless, were eventually embodied in the constitutional arrangements advanced by Britain's Colonial Secretary Ian Macleod in 1961. This resulted in the formation of the House of Chiefs in 1962. In that year, too, Macleod's proposals gave birth to a new constitution under which UNIP and ANC won elections and formed a coalition government. They thus broke the backbone of the hated Federation of Rhodesia and Nyasaland, finally setting the stage for the attainment of full political sovereignty on 24th October 1964.[73]

Conclusion

In African historiography, there is very little appreciation of the role traditional authorities played in the liberation struggles of the 1950s and 1960s. Their involvement of in the struggle for freedom has thus not been fully documented. This is partly because the emergence of independent states in the continent has chiefly been conceptualised as the consequence of the struggle for political freedom by a handful of Western-educated,

---

[71] Mulford, *Zambia*, p. 181.

[72] On this topic see Olajide Aluko, "Politics of decolonisation in British West Africa, 1945-1960," in J. F. Ade Ajayi and Michael Crowder (eds.), *History of West Africa* Vol. Two (Essex: Longman Group Ltd., 19), pp. 626-627.

[73] The most detailed study of the 1962 constitution is David C. Mulford, *The Northern Rhodesia Constitution* (Nairobi: Oxford University Press, 1964).

urban-based and politically sophisticated elite. Unsurprisingly, popular and academic discourse places a great premium upon such leading nationalists as Kenneth Kaunda of Zambia and Kwame Nkrumah of Ghana, depicting them as the true champions of African independence. Such leaders are said to have effectively exploited the urban discontent that unemployment and falling standards of living after the Second World War engendered. These conditions, it is argued, enabled leading urban-based nationalists to successfully pioneer militant mass politics and to whip up anti-colonial sentiments across Africa.[74] From this perspective, the struggle for political freedom was less a rural affair than an urban phenomenon dominated by a few politically skilled elites.

It is not difficult to see why most analysts of the politics of decolonisation in Africa have placed a premium on national-level freedom fighters. In most parts of the continent, it was, as Thomas Rasmussen observes, these leaders who challenged the ideology of colonialism, who articulated the demands for independence within and beyond the borders of European colonies, who pioneered mass politics, and dominated the highest positions in political parties.[75] The nationalist elite were further typically eager to write about their grievances, the strength of their political organisations, and their hopes for the future of the states they wanted to forge.[76] Thus, such men and women left behind a huge mine of information that usually eulogises their own role in the freedom struggle.[77] The image of these figures as political conquistadors was further unwittingly reinforced by European colonial officials. Across Africa, these functionaries often exaggerated the role high-level nationalists played in the struggle, while portraying rural dwellers as simple-minded folks who were not averse to colonial rule.[78]

But the struggle for independence in Africa was not a purely an elite or urban phenomenon. By examining the role the Chewa Paramount Chief played during the struggle for independence in colonial Zambia, this chapter suggests an alternative interpretation. Its central argument is that Kalonga Gawa Undi X and, of course other rural-based traditional authorities,

---

[74] See Cherry Gertzel and Morris Szeftel, "Politics in an African Urban Setting: The Role of the Copperbelt in the Copperbelt in the Transition to the One-Party State, 1964-1973," in Cherry Gertzel, Carolyn Baylies and Morris Szeftel (eds.), *The Dynamics of the One-Party State in Zambia* (Manchester: Manchester University Press, 1984).

[75] Thomas Rasmussen, "The popular basis of anti-colonial protest," in Tordoff (ed.), *Politics in Zambia*, pp. 40-41.

[76] Ibid.

[77] Ibid.

[78] Ibid.

played a central role in the mobilisation of anti-colonial forces in rural colonial Zambia. More than the urban-based elite, he and other traditional rulers were in a better position to comprehend their followers' grievances and to articulate such grievances through nationalist discourse. In this way, they transformed nationalist politics into a major rural concern, a task for which Kalonga Gawa Undi X in particular was pre-eminently qualified.

Not only was the Chewa ruler conversant with local political discourse and intrigue. He also effectively utilised such knowledge and existing social and political networks to advance the cause of political liberation, articulating this cause through familiar or familiarised idioms and institutions. Thus, he facilitated the assimilation of African nationalism at the grassroots level much more effectively than "outside agitators", whom most writers have placed at the centre of the politics of independence.[79] In the same vein, he embedded the fight for independence within prevailing social relations. Consequently, Kalonga Gawa Undi X attracted to the nationalist fold numerous followers, including his subordinate chiefs with their followers. The Paramount Chief, therefore, contributed in no small measure toward strengthening the crusade against British political hegemony. Through enlisting mass support for the crusade, he added his and his subjects' voice to the shrill demand for freedom from British supremacy. After the late 1950s, the British and European settlers in Zambia could ill-afford to ignore that voice.

What is most striking is that the traditional leader marshalled popular support against imperial subjugation through colonial institutions. Notable among these were Native Authorities and the Council of Chiefs. Paradoxically, it was through such institutions that colonial rulers hoped to counteract African nationalism in order to defend their hegemony. Moreover, whereas national-level nationalists themselves fought hard to undermine these institutions in order to weaken the colonial state, the Paramount Chief of the Chewa operated through them to attain a similar end. In so doing, the chief sought also to protect the chiefly office from the rising authoritarianism of African nationalists. Even more ironically, he deployed these very institutions to foster economic development among his followers before independence. After 1964, he would similarly transform the House of Chiefs, which outlived colonialism, into an

---

[79] See Cherry Gertzel and Morris Szeftel, "Politics in an African Urban Setting: "The Role of the Copperbelt in the Transition to the One-Party State, 1964-1973," in Cherry Gertzel, Carolyn Baylies and Morris Szeftel (eds.), *The Dynamics of the One-Party State in Zambia* (Manchester: Manchester University Press, 1984), pp. 118-122.

instrument for promoting national integration, contesting UNIP hegemonic agenda, and reining in political malcontents. It is to these themes that the next chapter turns.

4

An Ambiguous Agenda

Introduction

As intimated in the previous chapter, popular discourse rightly acknowledges the significant role Kalonga Gawa Undi X played in the liberation of colonial Zambia from British political domination. But the architects of this discourse have seldom explored the equally vital part that the Paramount Chief performed in shaping the country's economic destiny before and after 1964. Similarly, they have hardly grappled with his contribution toward influencing Zambia's political trajectory after the country attained independence. This has created the erroneous impression that the involvement of the traditional ruler in the creation of modern Zambia was confined to the politics of liberation alone and expired with the eradication of British political dominance in 1964.

It is grossly misleading to think that during the struggle for freedom Kalonga Gawa Undi X was only interested in the politics of decolonisation. Nor did his involvement in politics and other affairs of national significance cease after Zambia's independence. The present chapter seeks to explore the contributions of the sovereign towards the economic development of the territory both prior to and after 1964. It further examines his political thought and praxis in the aftermath of independence up to 1972, when Zambia became a one-party state. We argue that Kalonga Gawa Undi X was not only an agent of economic modernity. Politically speaking, after 1964 he was as much opposed to the surviving bastions of white settler supremacy in neighbouring territories as he was against internal government legislation that threatened to curtail chiefly authority, prestige and power. We show that although the Paramount Ruler continued to be an active ally of the first and successive post-colonial regimes in Zambia who endorsed thier economic and political policies, he, nonetheless, strove to wrest a measure of autonomy for the chiefly institution from the indifferent regimes. At the same time, he turned into an opponent of exclusive politics of ethnicity that crept into the country's political space as the ruling elites jockeyed for power and wealth, consequently threatening national integration, unity, and stability.

Few people would doubt that the Paramount Chief was a close ally of successive Zambian governments, the first of which was led by President Kenneth Kaunda. However, even though the traditional ruler supported the governments, his attitude toward them was at best ambivalent and ambiguous. He refused to be silenced whenever these governments passed legislation that he perceived as inimical to the welfare of the country and to chiefly authority and prerogatives. Kalonga Gawa Undi X, for instance, was as vehemently opposed to legislation that sought to undermine the authority of chiefs as he strenuously fought against what he perceived as societal evils, including regionalism, sectionalism, and politics of exclusion. In this vein, the Paramount Chief not infrequently castigated Zambian leaders whom he believed to be enemies of political unity. Prior to his death in 2004, Kalonga Gawa Undi X, as indicated in the next chapter, also embraced President Levy Mwanawasa's crusade against corruption that had become rampant under Zambia's second President, Frederick Jacob Titus Chiluba. In spite of his ambiguous stance towards successive regimes in Zambia, the Paramount Chief, nonetheless, continued to be consulted by the top leaders in the country on matters of national significance well up to his death.[1] This is a good measure of the high esteem in which they held the indefatigable old warrior.

"One cannot wage war on an empty stomach"

It is misleading to perceive the contribution of the Chewa potentate to the construction of Zambia as having been restricted to the political arena and to the colonial era alone. Long before and after independence, Kalonga Gawa Undi X remained committed to improving the welfare of his subjects. This commitment found vivid expression in his willingness to implement a host of economic reforms designed by colonial authorities after the Second World War. The commitment was also embedded in his warm endorsement of Zambia's post-colonial economic plans. To fully appreciate the role the traditional leader played in fostering economic development after independence, it is imperative first of all to underscore his attitude to economic

---

[1] In 2003, Gawa Undi X was, for example, one of the chiefs the Zambian government asked to make their contributions to the debate on the revision of the Land Act. See *Times of Zambia* 18 May 2003.

policies pursued by European authorities after the Second World War.

As many keen analysts have observed, post-war economic reforms in British Africa and beyond were part and parcel of the empire-wide economic plans under which Britain hoped to rebuild her war-ravaged economy at home.[2] With specific reference to colonial Zambia, these policies were intended to expand copper production and to stimulate rural food production in order to feed the growing population in the mining industry on the Zambian Copperbelt. Through this double-edged strategy Britain could improve the health of the colonised and, at the same time, turn the colony into a source of copper and other raw materials for the metropole. In trying to raise rural agricultural production, imperial authorities in the United Kingdom and colonial Zambia further hoped to raise the living standards for the growing African urban population and, thus, stem the rising tide of African resentment against the Federation of Rhodesia and Nyasaland.[3]

In rural colonial Zambia, post-war economic development plans were embodied in the agricultural policies that the colonial state pursued from 1945 to 1963. Collectively, these policies were designed to boost crop and livestock production through the introduction of scientific farming methods, resettlement schemes, optimal utilisation and conservation of natural resources, and adoption of technical skills.[4] The reforms under which imperial authorities sought to raise rural productivity after 1945 deeply resonated with the Paramount Chief's own desire to uplift the socio-economic welfare of his people via peasant commodity production. Thus, long before and after Kalonga Gawa Undi X joined the fight for freedom, he was an enthusiastic supporter of the imperial drive to promote modern farming in the colony. Like the colonial authorities, he enjoined his followers to abandon traditional farming methods and to convert to modern technologies of farming: crop rotation, controlled bush-burning, and contour farming to conserve soil fertility. Lastly, the Chewa ruler urged his subjects to attend agricultural shows annually in order to learn new ways of farming.[5]

---

[2] Samuel N. Chipungu, *The State, Technology and Peasant Differentiation in Zambia: A Case Study of Southern Province, 1930-1986* (Lusaka: Historical Association of Zambia, 1988), Chapter IV and Mebbiens Chewe Chabatama, "Peasant Farming, the State, and Food Security in North-Western Province of Zambia, 1902-1964," PhD dissertation: University of Toronto, 1999 and Tiyambe Zeleza, "The Political Economy of British Colonial Development and Welfare in British Africa," *TransAfrican Journal of History* 15 (1985), pp. 139-161.

[3] After the Second World War, Britain designed many schemes to win the political support of the nascent African elite. Peter Calvocoressi, *World Politics since 1945* (London and New York: Longman, 1991, first published in 1968).

[4] Chipungu, *State, Technology and Peasant Differentiation.*

[5] NAZ SEC 2/705, Katete Tour Report No 2 of 1951; NAZ EP 1/1/13, Katete Development Area Headquarters Quarterly Report, 31 March 1952.

The Paramount Chief's devotion to promoting improved commodity production in chiefdoms under his jurisdiction became particularly visible early in his career. During the familiarisation tours alluded to in the previous chapter, he routinely urged his subordinate chiefs to be at the centre of the spread of scientific animal husbandry and to enforce government soil conservation orders, including contour ridging, locally known as *mizere*. Kalonga Gawa Undi X took advantage of the meetings he held with chiefs and their subjects during the tours to stress the value of peasant commodity production. And, to this end, he defied the nationalist rhetoric of the African National Congress and in the United National Independence Party that urged rural dwellers to undermine post-war economic reforms in order to mock and to subvert the authority of the colonial state.

The sovereign led by practical example. By the end of the 1950s, he himself possessed a farm of not less than 100 acres at his Nyaviombo palace at Chiparamba near Chipata, where he mostly grew maize as a cash crop. He also possessed a smaller farm near his second palace at Mkaika in Katete, where he pioneered and popularised the cultivation of cash crops, notably Turkish tobacco and maize.[6] On both farms, the Paramount Chief was conscientiously devoted to scientific agriculture. As indicated above, he also repeatedly encouraged his subjects to turn to improved agriculture, and, to this end, he backed the efforts of the colonial state to engage local Native Authorities in the crusade to promote peasant commodity production. By the late 1950s, Kalonga Gawa Undi X had successfully prevailed upon Chewa Native Authorities at Nyaviombo, Chipili and Kagoro to enact orders under which offenders against soil conservation and other similar offences were either imprisoned for three months or fined between £1 and £2.[7]

The post-war agricultural plans that the Chewa overlord actively enforced produced mixed results in his chiefdoms. At a personal level, the enterprising leader himself and other chiefs apparently succeeded in taking market production to higher heights. This assertion finds support in the fact that Kalonga Gawa Undi X and most of his subordinate chiefs in Chewa Native Authorities evidently joined the class of "improved farmers". Unlike less successful segments of the rural peasantry in the province in the late 1950s and early 1960s, this category of producers possessed a large number of ploughs, scotch-carts, grinding mills, and, in the case of the

---

[6] Interview with Mama Nyangu, Mkaika, Katete, 12 November 2005.
[7] NAZ EP 1/1/36, Kuunika No 3 of 1957.

Paramount Chief, even tractors.[8] They sold more bags of maize, owned gramophones, and lived in bigger houses. They also demonstrated their penchant for modernity by the wearing European-style suits, driving luxury cars, and sending their sons and daughters to mission and government schools.[9] The prosperity of the chiefs in Superior Chewa Native Authority in particular may be gauged from the fact that in 1957 alone, they spent £450 on enlarging the Appeal Court at Nyaviombo, a very substantial amount in those days.[10] By the 1960s, the three Native Authorities under Kalonga Gawa Undi X owned so many herds of cattle that they were exporting livestock in and outside the Eastern province. They used the proceeds from this enterprise to purchase furniture for schools run by the Native Authorities.[11]

The growing prosperity of the Paramount Chief together with his subordinates extended to other commodity producers in the province. This was especially true in Chiefs Mbangombe and Kawaza's areas in Katete district, where the first agricultural resettlement schemes were established in the 1950s. In 1954, farmers in Chief Kawaza's area alone, produced 12,162 bags of maize and marketed 1,515 bags of shelled groundnuts, although the area was one of the strongholds of ANC which opposed resettlement schemes and other colonial economic reforms.[12] By 1957, Chief Mbang'ombe's area had become as a leading producer of maize, and Katete district the "workshop of development" in the province.[13]

In upholding the post-war economic agenda, Kalonga Gawa Undi X contributed in no small way toward the emergence of a class of rural producers in eastern Zambia prior to independence. Like other rural cultivators, these market producers were not immune to the vagaries of nature, to fluctuations in producer prices, inadequate marketing facilities, and, most importantly, to the discriminatory pricing policies that favoured European settler farmers above African peasants. It is not surprising, then, that by the late 1950s and 1960s, peasant commodity producers in Katete particularly were articulating their grievances linked to discrim-

---

[8] Mama Nyangu, interview cited.

[9] By 1954 Gawa Undi X himself owned a car. See NAZ EP4/7/13, Paramount Chief Undi to District Commissioner, 19 March 1954.

[10] NAZ SEC 2/710, Katete Tour Report No 5 of 1957.

[11] NAZ 1/1/19, Record of a meeting of the Chipili Sub-Council of the Chewa Native Authority held at Chadiza on the 25th March 1960.

[12] NAZ SEC 2/708, Katete Tour Report No 2/ 1954.

[13] Northern Rhodesia, African Affairs Annual Report for the Year 1957, p. 70.

inatory policies through nationalist rhetoric.[14] In so doing, they reinforced the struggle waged by both the ANC and UNIP against racist economic policies, the alienation of land to white farmers around Chipata, and the colonial state's failure to build roads and other economic infrastructure essential to boosting rural agriculture.[15] Peasant commodity producers thus raised the heat against colonial misrule.

Outside Katete district, agricultural progress seems to have been less spectacular. This was a consequence of a multiplicity of factors not least of which were the lack of marketing and transport facilities and, more significantly, stiff opposition from the local people against new methods of agriculture, especially contour ridging and crop rotation.[16] As intimated earlier, opposition to government-sponsored agricultural was largely orchestrated by the ANC and UNIP. In view of the fact that Kalonga Gawa Undi X himself actively championed colonial agricultural policies which both parties opposed, it is pertinent to explain why relations between him and the two political parties did not stretch to a breaking point over these policies. This question is all the more essential because top leaders in ANC and UNIP dismissed chiefs who enforced the agricultural policies of the colonial state after 1945 as no more than government bootlickers or stooges.

It is puzzling that Kalonga Gawa Undi X was apparently not one of the victims of such finger-pointing, even though he openly implemented post-war agricultural plans. The answer to the paradox may partly lie in the fact that by the time the ANC and later UNIP increased the heat against colonial economic policies in the late 1950s and early 1960s, the Chewa Sovereign was already as wholly committed to dismantling the colonial apparatus as were leading nationalist elites at national and grassroots level. It would appear that party activists were unwilling to alienate the support of such a valuable ally by exerting on him and his Native Authorities undue political pressure over the policies in question. His unquestionable loyalty to the liberation cause thus enabled him to escape the pressure the ANC and UNIP exerted on other traditional rulers outside his chiefdoms. Indeed, in the Luapula and Northern provinces such pressure was so intense that it completely paralysed colonial development initiatives after the Second

14 NAZ SEC 2/ 712, Katete Tour Report No 11 of 1959.
15 For an engaging debate on this topic, see MacDixon-Fyle, "The Seventh Day Adventists (S.D.A) in the Protest Politics of the Tonga Plateau, Northern Rhodesia," *African Social Research* 26 (1978), pp. 453-467; Jotham C. Momba, "Peasant Differentiation and Rural Party Politics in Colonial Zambia," *Journal of Southern African Studies* 11, 2 (1985), pp. 281-294; Chipungu, *State, Technology and Peasant Differentiation*.
16 See NAZ SEC 2/710, Katete Tour Report No 5 of 1957; on the same file see Katete Tour Report No 11 of 1957.

World War.[17] Left unmolested by nationalist political actors, the suzerain enjoyed sufficient space to advance scientific agriculture in keeping with his dream to boost the economic welfare of his followers. This enabled him to make true his adage that the freedom struggle in the colony could not successfully be waged "on an empty stomach".[18]

Just as the engagement of the Chief with liberation politics survived the attainment of independence in 1964, as demonstrated below, so did his interest in bolstering rural economic development. Successive governments in post-colonial Zambia therefore found him a willing ally in their effort to co-opt traditional authorities in rural development schemes. Thus, for example, from 1965 when Kalonga Gawa Undi X sat in the Fort Jameson (Chipata) Rural District Council (of which he became Secretary in 1967) and from 1968 to 1981 when he served as the Chairman of the House of Chiefs, he played a no minor role in the creation of government-sponsored Village, District, and Provincial Development Committees. As the Chief himself observed in 1965, it was through these institutions that the post-colonial regime hoped to raise standards of living in rural areas, and to implement its First and Second Five Year Development Plans.[19] To encourage the creation of development committees, he personally held meetings across the length and breadth of his chiefdoms, enjoining his subjects to form and enlist in the committees apparently with considerable success.[20] At the same time, Kalonga Gawa Undi X chaired several meetings of the Standing Committee of the Provincial Council of Chiefs in Chipata. At these meetings, he unfailingly cajoled other traditional rulers together with their subjects to play their "fullest part in cooperating with the Government in promoting the National Development of the Republic of Zambia".[21]

The success that attended the Paramount Chief's campaign to create development committees and raise productivity after independence may be partly gauged from the agility with which such committees were established the mid-1960s onwards in chiefdoms under his control.[22] More

---

17 See Mulford, Zambia.

18 Mama Nyangu, interview cited.

19 NAZ EP 1/154, Paramount Chief Undi to District Secretaries, Lundazi and Petauke, 13 March 1965.

20 Interview with Alick Chifunya Phiri, Headman, Kafumbwe village 08 August 2008.

21 NAZ EP 1/1/54, minutes of the Standing Committee of the Eastern Province Council of Chiefs held in the Board Room on Thursday 9 February 1967. On the same file see Address to chiefs by President of the House of Chiefs on 12 November 1971. See also NAZ 4/10/18, Provincial seminar held at Chizongwe Secondary School on 21-22 April 1967.

22 See NAZ EP 1/1/62, Minutes of the Fort Jameson Council meeting held at Feni on Thursday 30th-31st March 1965; NAZ EP 4/1/98, Record of the Provincial Development Committee meeting held in the rural council chamber on 18th January 1969.

concretely, it may be discerned in the rising numbers of peasant farmers in areas under his sway.[23] In 1969, Chewa chiefdoms in Katete district alone boasted 2,500 farmers. Between them, these farmers received loans worth K86,000, no mean figure in those days.[24] There are indications, too, that his efforts to engage his followers in commodity production after independence contributed to the consolidation of cash cropping in Eastern province, with the overlord himself as one of the region's leading market producers. This observation vindicates the assertion that the role of the Paramount Chief in the configuration of modern Zambia transcended his involvement in nationalist politics. He was as equally instrumental in liberating the country from the vestiges of foreign rule as he sought to free it from the depravations of poverty, with its offshoots of disease, hunger and malnutrition.

Politics after Independence

The commitment of the Chewa ruler to raising agricultural production after independence was paralleled by an ambiguous posture in which he supported President Kenneth Kaunda's regime but, at the same time, condemned its excesses, especially its propensity to emasculate chiefly authority and power. Kalonga Gawa Undi X also spared no effort to discredit members of the ruling elite, whose political machinations he perceived as inimical to the stability and unity of the country. These assertions find evidence in how the Paramount Chief reacted to a number of major events, external and internal, that took place between 1965 and 1971. Specifically, these were the imposition of the Unilateral Declaration of Independence (UDI) by Ian Smith in colonial Zimbabwe (formerly Rhodesia) in 1965, the enactment of the Local Government and Local Courts Acts by the Zambian government in the same year, and, lastly, the formation of the United Progressive Party (UPP) by Simon Mwansa Kapwepwe in 1971, which posed the greatest threat to the political hegemony UNIP had enjoyed since independence.

That Kalonga Gawa Undi X was a committed political ally of the first post-colonial regime in Zambia is perhaps best aptly exemplified by his response toward Ian Smith's proclamation of the UDI in neighbouring colonial Zimbabwe in 1965. An illegal act which has spawned a veritable

---

[23] On the creation of development committees, see NAZ EP4/1/106, Minutes of the Chiefs' meeting held in the Rural Chambers on 16 January 1970 at 8.50 AM.

[24] NAZ EP 4/1/1/98, The record of minutes of the District Development Committee held at Katete Court room on 24 February 1969 at 9.00 AM.

research industry of its own, the UDI was anathema to Zambia's declared commitment to annihilate the surviving the bastions of white settler supremacy in southern Africa.[25] To emasculate this commitment and the support Zambia rendered to liberation movements against white domination, Smith closed Zambia's southern routes to the sea on which the country traditionally relied for its exports and imports. He also threatened to blow up the Kariba Hydro-power station to cut off the country's most important source of electric power for its mining industry and thus derail economic development. This grossly compromised the young nation's economic security.

Smith's retaliatory measures worried Kalonga Gawa Undi X, not to mention President Kaunda and other top leaders. Nonetheless, the Paramount Chief openly backed the President's uncompromising stand against white minority rule in Rhodesia and beyond. In endorsing this stand, he entered the political fray against the Smith regime. Addressing the House of Chiefs on 9 December 1965, he eloquently spoke against the Unilateral Declaration of Independence, maintaining that the principles of democracy that Zambians cherished most required them to buttress President Kaunda's condemnation of "the seizure of independence by the rebel regime in Rhodesia". Like Kenneth Kaunda, the traditional ruler believed that the UDI was treasonable. He, therefore, supported Kaunda's call upon the British government to quell the rebellion in Rhodesia by military force.[26] The militant stand of the Paramount Chief against the UDI coupled with his earlier role in the combat against colonial domination was highly appreciated by the Zambian government and President Kaunda in 1966. In that year, the President conferred upon the Paramount Chief the honour of the Officer of Distinguished service (O.D.S.).[27] If the bold stand of the old warrior endeared him to Kenneth Kaunda, it also received warm support from within the House of Chiefs. This evidently emboldened Kaunda in his resolve to bring down the illegal regime in the nearby colony at any cost.

But the warm feelings between the Zambian government and the traditional ruler that issued over the UDI saga in colonial Zimbabwe soon began to evaporate. Cracks and crevices began to appear in the relationship

[25] For a detailed eyewitness account of the Unilateral Declaration of Independence, see Robert C. Good, U.D.I.: *The International Politics of the Rhodesian Rebellion* (London: Faber and Faber, 1973). For Zambia's reaction to the UDI, consult Richard L. Sklar, "Zambia's response to the Rhodesian unilateral declaration of independence," in William Tordoff (ed.), *Politics in Zambia* (Manchester: Manchester University Press, 1975), pp. 320-362.

[26] NAZ EP 1/1/54, Minutes of the Ninth Meeting of the House of Chiefs, 9th December 1965.

[27] Gawa Undi X, "Speech".

between the two parties even before the death knell of the UDI sounded, mainly because of Kaunda's unwillingness to make good his enthusiastic promise in the early 1960s that traditional rulers' authority, prerogatives, and power would be safeguarded after the ascent of the United National Independence Party to the political throne. The roots of the tensions between Kalonga Gawa Undi X and the post-colonial regime lay deep in the administrative reforms the Kaunda-led government instituted soon after independence. From President Kaunda's stand point, these reforms were meant to strengthen the facade of the central government and to rationalise the operations of Native Authorities. To the Chewa leader and other traditional authorities across Zambia, however, these reforms were no more than political manoeuvres by which the new ruling class sought to monopolise power at the expense of chiefly authority, prestige, and prerogatives.

Among the earliest reforms that strained relations between the government and the Paramount Chief was a fiscal reform introduced just a few months after independence. The reform abolished the old practice under which chiefs and councillors' subsidies were paid by Native Authorities. Under the new reform all recognised traditional rulers across the newly-independent nation were to be paid subsidies at fixed minimum and maximum rates determined by central government. The UNIP government defended this arrangement on the ground that it ensured uniformity in the emoluments chiefs received across the country. However, since the amount of chiefly emoluments in the pre-independence era depended largely on the level of the prosperity of each Native Authority, this fiscal reform resulted in drastic reduction of some traditional rulers' subsidies. Among the most adversely affected by the new monetary arrangement were particularly chiefs who had earlier presided over wealthy Native Authorities. Many chiefs, with Kalonga Gawa Undi X prominent among them, thus inevitably perceived the payment of uniform subsidies as an assault upon their fiscal independence, their prestige, and hence their own role in independent Zambia.[28]

Their apprehensions were soon justified. Before the close of the year of independence, President Kenneth Kaunda demonstrated his determination to pay little more than lip service to the prestige of traditional rulers. In that year, his government announced its intention to take away chiefs' administrative and judicial powers and functions on the pretext that this would

---

[28] See NAZ EP 1/154, Record of a meeting held in the Conference Room at Fort Jameson on 5th January 1964. On the same file see also, Notes on meeting between the Vice-President and Eastern Province Chief held at Fort Jameson on Wednesday 9th June 1965.

place them above partisan politics. To this end, and in spite of stiff resistance from chiefs country-wide, the President introduced in parliament the controversial Local Government Bill in 1965. This Bill was designed to supplant Native Authorities with a system of elected local authorities throughout the country.[29] A year later, the UNIP government further sought to pass in parliament the Local Courts Bill to make good its earlier threat to remove traditional rulers from presiding over local courts, a function they had performed since the establishment of Native Courts in the 1930s.[30]

The legislative onslaught of the Kaunda's regime on the prerogatives and power of traditional rulers did not escape the wrath of traditional authorities in the country. With the writing visible on the wall, Kalonga Gawa Undi X, for example, typically went on the offensive to protect the chiefly office. Much as he had earlier utilised Native Authorities and the Council of Chiefs to advance the anti-imperial crusade, the Chewa Paramount Chief now enlisted the House of Chiefs in his crusade against both the Local Courts and Local Government Bills. To this end, he and Chief Mapanza, the first President of the House of Chiefs, effectively used the House to sensitise other chiefs across the country against legislative machinations that sought to emasculate their power and the authority.[31]

Led by Kalonga Gawa Undi X and Chief Mapanza, Provincial Councils of Chiefs country-wide raised a huge storm of protest over both Bills throughout the mid-1960s. In the Eastern province, the District Secretary, R. S. Thompson, observed in 1966 that local authorities in the Provincial Council who represented other chiefs in the House of Chiefs campaigned vigorously against the Bills.[32] One of such campaigners was Chief Mphamba of the Tumbuka people in Lundazi district. A close ally of the Chewa Paramount Chief in the Eastern Province Council of Chief and in the House of Chiefs, Mphamba perhaps best expressed other chiefs' indignation over the two Bills. "It is ridiculous," the Tumbuka ruler angrily told the House of Chiefs in 1966, "to see that the Party [i.e. UNIP] we supported [during the liberation struggle] is turning against us. Rural areas are for chiefs. [But]

---

[29] NAZ EP 1/1/54, Minutes of the Ninth Meeting of the House Chiefs 9th December 1965.

[30] For a fuller treatment of this topic see, Kusum Datta, "The Policy of Indirect Rule in Zambia (Northern Rhodesia), 1924-1953," PhD dissertation: University of London, 1976; Ben Kakoma, "Colonial Administration in North-Western Rhodesia: A Case Study of Administration in the Mwinilunga District, 1900-1939," M.A. dissertation: University of Auckland, 1971.

[31] NAZ EP 1/1/54, Paramount Chief Undi to District Commissioner, Chipata, 3 March 1965, Nyaviombo Palace. On the same file see, Paramount Chief Undi to District Secretary, Chipata, 12 April 1965.

[32] NAZ EP 1/1/54, R. S. Thompson, District Secretary to Resident Secretary, 21 May 1966.

[w]e have seen two Bills which completely ignore us, the Local Courts Bill and the Local Authority Bill…. We are told that we [chiefs] are administrators, but what do we administrate?" The visibly upset chief accused the UNIP-led government of betraying the trust chiefs vested in it.[33]

Likewise, Kalonga Gawa Undi X, in his capacity as the first Secretary of the Provincial Council of Chiefs in Eastern Province and later as the Vice-Chairman and Chairman of the House of Chiefs in Lusaka, added his own chorus to condemning the Bills in question. He dismissed both Bills as no more than UNIP's ploy to break the power of chiefs in the country. At the same time, the Paramount Chief wondered what the work of the chiefs would be if these Bills were passed as law in parliament. He implored all the recognised chiefs in and outside the Eastern province to speak with one voice in condemning the Bills.[34] In roundly castigating the proposed legislation and the Acts that they eventually spawned, the Chewa sovereign and other chiefs asserted their right to political autonomy. They thus strongly refused to be politically marginalised.

But all their protests fell on deaf ears. In 1965 and 1966, the UNIP government, which often piously declared that chiefs in independent Zambia would continue to be the "fathers of their people," passed both Bills over their loud protests. These Acts widened the fissure in the relations between the government and traditional leaders, and grossly contributed to the erosion of chiefly power, authority and prestige. That chiefly authority and prestige sharply declined in the aftermath of independence is adequately attested by the suspension of the meetings of the House of Chiefs by the Zambian government for more than a decade before Kalonga Gawa Undi X passed away in 2004.[35]

Tensions between the potentate and the UNIP-controlled government did not reach a breaking point, despite the Chief's ire over the politically debilitating legislation. This is vividly instanced by his devotion to the government's policy aimed at promoting economic development and safeguarding national unity and political stability. As suggested by his militant stand against the UDI, Kalonga Gawa Und X also backed the government in defending the country's hard-won independence and unity from external threats after 1964. But he was also equally concerned with nipping in

---

[33] NAZ EP 1/1/54, Republic of Zambia, Minutes of the 10th Meeting of the House of Chiefs, 4th April 1966.
[34] NAZ EP 1/1/54, Paramount Chief Undi to Paramount Chief Mpezeni III, OBE, 23 December 1964; on the same file, see Minutes of the Ninth Meeting of the House of Chiefs, 9th December 1966.
[35] See *Times of Zambia*, 13 April 2003.

the bud disruptive internal forces that began to erode national unity and cohesion soon after independence.

These internal forces, particularly regionalism and tribalism, have, like the UDI, been a subject of extensive academic research, and therefore, need not detain us here for too long.[36] It is important to note, however, that both regionalism and tribalism had been simmering beneath the surface of the nationalist struggle during the struggle for freedom, and deepened with growing sectional rivalries within the ruling party after 1964. These problems found expression in the creation of ethnically-driven political parties such as the Lozi-dominated United Party in 1966 and later, as shown below, the United Progressive Party (UPP) allegedly dominated by Bemba-speaking politicians. Both regionalism and sectionalism reared their ugly head in intense in-fighting within the ruling party, as politicians jostled for jobs, for influential political positions and power. This political rivalry threatened not only to tear UNIP itself apart but the nation as whole. In February 1968, these divisive forces indeed deepened so much that they compelled President Kenneth Kaunda to resign for a few hours. As eyewitnesses have more recently observed, this raised the spectre of inter-ethnic bloodshed in the country.[37]

Matters came to a head in 1971 when Simon Mwansa Kapwepwe, claiming that the Bemba were marginalized in both UNIP and its government, broke away from the governing party to form UPP.[38] Reportedly dominated by Bemba-speakers, the new political party posed the greatest threat to UNIP's political ascendancy and hegemony since its formation in 1959. Both parties unsurprisingly soon became locked in bloody confrontations that left behind increasing cases of muggings, murder and arson, especially on the Zambian Copperbelt. Kalong Gawa Undi X, now a seasoned politician, saw the jostling for power between and within political parties on the basis of regionalism and sectionalism as a grave danger to the spirit of nationalism that had unified all Zambians during the

---

[36] For good examples of studies on this topic, see Richard Hall, *The High Price of Principles: Kaunda and the White South* (London: Hodder and Stoughton, 1969) and Robert Molteno, "Cleavage and conflict in Zambian politics: a study in sectionalism," William Tordoff (ed.), *Politics in Zambia*, pp. 62-106.

[37] See Sikota Wina, The Night Without a President (Lusaka: Multimedia, 1985); see also Alexander Grey Zulu, *Memoirs of Alexander Grey Zulu* (Ndola: Printpak, 2007).

[38] For a fuller and most recent study of the rise of the UPP, see Miles Larmer, "'A Little bit like a volcano': The United Progressive Party and Resistance to One-Party Rule in Zambia, 1964-1980," *International Journal of African Historical Studies*, 39 (2006) and his "Enemies within? Opposition to Zambian one-party state, 1972-1980," in Jan-Bart Gewald, Marja Hinfelaar and Giacomo Macola (eds), *One Zambia, Many Histories: Towards a History of Post-colonial Zambia* (Leiden and London: Brill, 2008), pp.98-128.

combat for independence. Worried that this would erode national integration, stability and economic prosperity, the Chewa chief became a relentless nemesis of national-level leaders who appealed to ethnic sentiments to advance their political ambitions or careers.

Characteristically, Kalonga Gawa Undi X turned to the House of Chiefs to register his and other chiefs' disapproval of politics of exclusion. With the House of Chiefs as his platform, he vehemently fought against ethnic politics, repeatedly voiced what he saw as chiefs' role in fostering national unity, and unfailingly often sounded a warning bell against UPP leaders and their sympathisers. The concerns of the Paramount Chief raised by politics of ethnicity are best illustrated by a lengthy and biting speech that he made as Chairman of the House of Chiefs against UPP at a meeting attended by President Kenneth Kaunda in Lusaka on 12 November 1971. The speech is worth quoting at length:

> It is generally accepted that we chiefs in Zambia are above politics. Nevertheless, I feel that we chiefs should be heard loud and clear whenever a situation that causes chaos in the country develops. We chiefs in Zambia are gravely concerned about the recent political tension now taking place in the nation. We wish to make our stand clear on this issue. All the chiefs in Zambia are happy with the progress and other developments which have been achieved under Your Excellency's wise leadership since Zambia became independent. I wish to make this point clear that much progress and material benefits we are witnessing have been accomplished because of peace and unity which have prevailed in the last seven years of independence.[39]

Kalonga Gawa Undi X feared that politics driven by sectionalism and regionalism would not only grossly undermine "the progress and material benefits" the country had achieved since independence. He also believed that divisive politics would lead to bloodletting, and he portrayed himself together with other traditional rulers as the custodians of Zambia's post-colonial achievements and peace:

> The Hon. Chiefs deeply regret that some people who were once upon a time among those who had fought for independence are now working day and night to destroy unity and thus put a 5 years break to the tremendous progress now taking place in the country. We love peace and

---

[39] NAZ EP 1/1/54, Address to the Chiefs by the President of House of Chiefs on 12 November 1971, p. 4.

pray that unity should prevail in Zambia. We therefore condemn the formation of the United Progressive Party which in our view will cause disturbances and bloodshed. We fear that the uncalled for activities of UPP will in the end result in the loss of lives of innocent people.[40]

Kalonga Gawa Undi X assured President Kaunda that to forestall bloodshed and foster economic development and harmony, traditional authorities in Zambia would solidly rally behind the President's efforts to curb the United Progressive Party:

We want to assure you Your Excellency that we are solidly behind you together with our people in our respective areas. We have no time for the self-styled pioneer and hungry politicians who are fighting for self-personal gains. We chiefs wish to add our voices to all Zambians who have the interest of the country at heart that the power hungry clicher [sic] of UPP should be stamped out in the interest of peace and harmony for economic development we so much desire. We have already won [the] independence we were fighting for. What remains now is for us all to plan together the next Second National Development Plan for this country. We do not want as chiefs that [the] independence we [have] already won be spoiled, confused [by] political litigants. We are pleased that you are handling the situation and that you are taking action against those power hungry [people] who wish to ruin the fruits of independence and who want to hinder the progress of the country.[41]

In this torrent of words may, retrospectively, be discerned the Paramount Chief's post-colonial political thought. In them, too, can be seen his ambivalent stance towards the Zambian government, and the associative links the traditional leader forged between the Kaunda-led regime and economic and political development in the aftermath of independence. To Kalong Gawa Undi X, the UNIP government plainly guaranteed political stability and economic prosperity. He, nonetheless, insisted that the government needed to heed the voice of traditional rulers on matters that affected the nation as a whole. That voice, the old nationalist maintained, had to be autonomous and respected by the governing political elite. Thus, even as late as November 1971, the old freedom fighter was still challenging the

---

[40] NAZ EP 1/1/54, Address to the Chiefs by the President of the House of Chiefs on 12 November 1971, p. 4

[41] NAZ EP 1/1/54, Address to the Chiefs by the President of the House of Chiefs 12 November 1971, pp. 4-5; see also NAZ EP1/1/55, Tour report of constituencies in Katete District by District Governor Mr. T.C. Maimisa, 8th-15th November 1971.

Photo 4 Kalonga Gawa Undi X addressing the House of Chiefs as Chairman, as former President Dr. Kenneth Kaunda and Vice-President Mainza Chona look on. Courtesy of National Archives of Zambia

propensity of the post-colonial state in Zambia to relegate chiefs to the background of politics by undermining their authority, power, and prerogatives. This confounded its efforts to push chiefs off the stage of national politics.

This notwithstanding, the Paramount Chief's lengthy verbal fusillade quoted above clearly shows that in the 1970s, Kalonga Gawa Undi X came to equate Zambia's political and economic prosperity with the continuity of the Kaunda-dominated regime in power. Indeed until the re-introduction of multi-party politics in the 1990s, the chief also held that only the UNIP government held the key to the preservation of national unity and integrative politics. It is in this context that one may perhaps appreciate his bitterness against UPP and other opposition parties, which he feared would erode political stability and economic prosperity in the country.

From this standpoint, it is possible to comprehend why the protagonist eagerly agreed to sit on the Constitutional Review Commission established by President Kaunda in 1971 to examine the question of turning Zambia into a one-party state. Henceforth, the suzerain became a tireless campaign-

74

er of the abolition of the multi-party system of governance that Zambia inherited at independence. To the Chewa ruler, as to other advocates of the one-party system of governance across independent Africa, this transition would usher in a golden era of national integration, peace, unity, and stability. Kalonga Gawa Undi X hoped that one-party politics would obviate the creation of ethnically or regionally-based parties such as Kapwepwe's UPP and Harry Nkumbula's ANC.[42] In his view, one party democracy would in turn leave no room for the rise of "self-styled and power-hungry politicians," whose central object was to further their own "self-personal gains".[43]

To the extent that the Paramount Chief actively supported the introduction of one-party system over the multi-party politics, political scientists and historians alike may judge him harshly. But sympathetic analysts reckoning with the political tensions, the beatings, the rising cases of arson and murder that gripped Zambia's early years of independence, would perhaps conclude that his campaign for the abandonment of multi-party politics was a mark of his statesmanship and faith in the virtue of integrative politics. To Kalonga Gawa Undi X, the one-party system provided an umbrella that would accommodate all Zambians irrespective of ethnic, linguistic, cultural and political backgrounds. This system of governance would, he hoped, reunite people as they had been during the struggle for independence. He, therefore, saw one-party rule as the surest path to strengthening national integration, unity and cohesion after the rise of the UPP in the early 1970s. Perhaps the old freedom fighter did not foresee that one-party politics would breed dictatorial tendencies such as the concentration of power in the presidency at the expense of other arms of government, an addiction from which the country has yet to recover to this day.[44]

Conclusion

Economically and politically, Kalonga Gawa Undi X was an enigmatic actor. During the struggle for independence, he actively campaigned for the dissolution of the British misrule in colonial Zambia. Yet this did not make him shy away from taking advantage of some post-war policies that he perceived as pivotal to uplifting the economic welfare of his subjects. To

---

[42] See Zulu, *Memoirs* , Chapters Thirty-three and Thirty-four.

[43] NAZ EP 1/1/54, Address to the Chiefs by the President of House of Chiefs on 12 November 1971, p. 5.

[44] For a captivating analysis of this issue, see Jan Van Donge, "Zambia, Kaunda and Chiluba: Enduring Patterns of Political Culture," in John A. Wiseman (ed.), *Democracy and Political Change in Sub-Saharan Africa* (London and New York: Routledge, 1995).

this end, he enthusiastically supported the agricultural initiatives introduced by colonial authorities to expand rural production in Africa after the Second World War. He did so boldly, in the face of stiff opposition from other nationalists, who saw the undermining of post-war agricultural schemes as a short step to annihilating colonial hegemony.

The traditional ruler carried over this ambiguous posture into the political space after Zambia gained independence in 1964. Although he undoubtedly supported the post-colonial government with its economic policies, he tenaciously fought against its efforts to eject traditional authorities from the political space and to undermine their power and prerogatives. This explains the stiff opposition the Chewa ruler and his counterparts in the House of Chiefs and the Council of Chiefs in the Eastern Province put up against the introduction of both the Local Government and Local Courts Act in 1965 and 1966, respectively. Although their protests against this legislation went unanswered, Kalonga Gawa Undi X stopped short of withdrawing his allegiance from Kaunda's regime. This is certainly because he believed that the regime guaranteed peace, unity, stability and economic development in the country. Needless to say, it was for this very reason that the old nationalist solidly rallied behind UNIP's call for the displacement of multi-party democracy with one-party rule in the 1970s. It was a decision the Paramount Chief would apparently later regret.

5

Contesting Economic and Political Woes

Introduction

The introduction of the one-party state in Zambia, which Kalonga Gawa Undi X indisputably welcomed in the 1970s, soon spawned despotism that the traditional ruler and other enthusiasts of the so-called one-party democracy did not earlier anticipate. Under one-party governance, political and economic power came to rest almost solely in the hands of the presidency at the expense of the other arms of the government. As President Kenneth Kaunda and his close lieutenants in the United National Independence Party (UNIP), increasingly monopolised power, the government correspondingly became inept, corrupt and less responsible to the electorate. The ruling elite ruthlessly silenced those unwilling to toe the party line. Among the casualties of UNIP undemocratic rule were traditional rulers, whose influence, power and prestige rapidly diminished as the Kaunda-controlled regime systematically pushed chiefs and political rivals out of the political space. In the absence of checks and balances, the government proved incapable of redressing the country's political, social, and economic woes that began to plague it after the prices of oil prices shot up and copper prices spiraled downward on the international market in the early 1970s.

This chapter attempts to explore the ways in which the Chewa traditional leader responded to these challenges from the early 1970s up to his death in 2004. It maintains that while the old nationalist undoubtedly continued to support the economic and foreign policies of the Kaunda-led government for most of this long period, he increasingly became discontented with its economic incompetence, its political intolerance, its monopoly over power, and its corruption. Apprehensive about the deteriorating economic situation in the country, the Paramount Chief turned into an advocate of self-help economic ventures. To this end, he, like the post-colonial regime, began to tackle poverty through cooperative societies and other self-help initiatives. In the late 1970s and 1980s, Kalonga Gawa Undi X vigorously campaigned for the creation of producer, consumer and marketing cooperatives throughout his chiefdoms. But despite his and the government's efforts to raise rural agricultural production through self-help initiatives, poverty escalated throughout the country; so did economic mismanagement and corruption in the high echelons of the UNIP administration. As the inability of the government to curb skyrocketing poverty and corruption became glaring, the veteran politician seems to have leaned towards the campaign for the re-introduction of multiparty politics in the late 1980s.[1] Simultaneously, he continued to wage his earlier crusade to regain the waning prestige, prerogatives, and power of traditional rulers. To this end, in 2003 he successfully lobbied the late President Levy Patrick Mwanawasa's government to revive the House of Chiefs, after it had been practically defunct for more than a decade. Finally, the Paramount Chief joined the anti-corruption fray launched by Levy Mwanawasa against the architects of the previous regime that had removed President Kaunda from office in 1991.

Zambia's Economic and Political Malaise

Zambia inherited a buoyant economy at independence in 1964. As Robert H. Bates rightly observes, the country, which barely a century earlier was predominantly an agricultural territory, had by the 1960s turned into one of the world's leading producers and exporters of copper.[2] With the commodity's prices on the international market being unprecedentedly favourable, Zambia's per capita gross domestic product (GDP) rose considerably to become one of the highest in the so-called developing world after independence. By 1969, the GDP in Zambia was two times higher than that of Egypt, three times that of Kenya, and, most unexpectedly, higher than even those of some middle-income countries, including South Korea, Brazil and Malaysia.[3] This wealth quickly rubbed off on to rural dwellers in the chiefdoms under Kalonga Gawa Undi X and across the country. In 1965, for example, the Fort Jameson Rural District Council in

---

[1] Interview with Edward Nyirongo, Grandson of Kalonga Gawa Undi X, Mkaika Palace, 13 November 2005.

[2] Robert H. Bates, *Rural Responses to Industrialization: A Study of Village Zambia* (New Haven: Yale University Press, 1976), p. 1.

[3] James Ferguson, *Expectations of Modernity: Myths and Meanings of Urban Life on the Zambian Copperbelt* (Berkeley, Los Angeles and London: University of California Press, 1999), p.6.

Eastern province embarked on unprecedented expansion of infrastructure and agriculture. Within Chewa chiefdoms, the Council in that year alone built or maintained roads in Kagoro at the cost of £805 and in Chadiza and Chiparamba at the cost of £400 and £350, respectively.[4] Working hand in hand with the Natural Resources Board, the Rural District Council further set up conservation committees to promote advanced farming.[5] The affluence of the newly independent country also manifested itself in the construction by the central government of numerous new schools, clinics, and hospitals throughout the province soon after independence.

But Zambia's robust economic bubble soon burst. The price of copper, which accounted for more than ninety per cent of the country's exports, plummeted sharply in the early 1970s and consequently copper production declined drastically. As if this was not enough, the middle of that decade witnessed an unprecedented rise in the cost of oil on the international market. The outcome of these developments was catastrophic for Zambia. The per capita income, for example, plummeted by more than fifty per cent from 1974 to 1991, with the gross national product (GNP) per capita falling by an average of 3.1 percent between 1980 and 1993.[6] By the latter date, Zambia, which had been one of the richest countries in the developing world in the 1960s, had become one of the poorest in the whole world. As James Ferguson remarks, by the early 1990s, fifty-five percent of the population in Zambia lived on incomes too inadequate to purchase basic nutritional requirements, while sixty-eight percent lived "in households with expenditures below a level sufficient to provide 'basic needs'".[7] As the economy declined, unemployment soared and shortages of basic foodstuffs like maize meal, salt, sugar, soap, and cooking oil became as rampant as queuing for the commodities.[8] Both mining and agriculture in the country virtually collapsed, leading to declining production, rising poverty, and unnerving crime, prostitution and HIV/AIDS.

Many observers have attributed Zambia's post-colonial economic woes to the fall in copper prices and to the rise in oil prices.[9] While there is

---

[4] NAZ EP 1/1/62, Minutes of the meeting of the Fort Jameson Rural Council held at Feni on 21-22 June 1965.

[5] See NAZ EP 1/1/63, P.R. Hall, Secretary, Natural Resources Board, to Secretary, Fort Jameson Council, 20 February 1965.

[6] Ferguson, *Expectations of Modernity*, p. 6.

[7] Ferguson, *Expectations of Modernity*, p. 6.

[8] See Jan-Bart Gewald, Marja Hinfelaar and Giacomo Macola, "Introduction," in Jan-Bart Gewald, Marja Hinfelaar and Giacomo Macola (eds.), *One Zambia, Many Histories: Towards a History of Post-colonial Zambia* (Leiden and London: Brill, 2008), pp. 2.

[9] For a recent exploration of some of the post-colonial policies that contributed to the collapse of the Zambian economy between 1968 and 1980, see Hugh Macmillan, "'The devil you know': The

much to be said in favour of this view, it is also undeniable that other forces ranging from economic mismanagement, corruption, political patronage to Zambia's costly support for liberation wars in southern Africa all left a devastating effect on the collapsing economy. Saddled with these difficulties, the UNIP government proved incapable of meeting the expectations of independence of the majority of Zambians. Inefficiency within the government itself shot up, corruption became rampant, rural agricultural production collapsed, and so did people's standard of living across the country. By the late 1970s, the UNIP leaders' inability to make good their pre-independence promises to Zambians was glaring, engendering widespread discontent in the country.[10] Unable to arrest their own incompetence coupled with growing popular discontent, the UNIP leaders became more despotic and less responsive to the needs of Zambians.[11] Concomitantly, competition for control of and corruption in the ruling party steadily mounted. To maintain their grip on power within this climate, the political elite increasingly exerted demands on the party's leading officials not only to divert the available meagre resources to their own constituents but also to appoint their supporters to the ever bulging state-controlled bureaucracy and companies.[12]

Combating Economic Woes

Reconstructing how Kalonga Gawa Undi X reacted to this unfolding social, economic and political scenario after 1972 is even more problematic than recreating his earlier ideologies and praxis. This arises from the dearth of data. As the authority of traditional rulers in Zambia rapidly diminished after the abolition of multi-party politics and UNIP monopolised power, the Paramount Chief himself seldom expressed in writing his views on national affairs, as he did before. Thus, what we know of his ideologies and experiences in the decades preceding his death mostly derives from oral sources with their attendant limitations highlighted earlier in this volume. Scanty press accounts supplement oral evidence. But written by journalists,

---

impact of the Mulungushi economic reforms on retail trade in rural Zambia, with specific reference to Susman Brothers & Wulfsohn, 1968-1980," in Gewald, Hinfelaar and Macola (eds), *One Zambia*, pp. 187-212.

10 This topic has recently been wittily analysed by Giacomo Macola, "'It means as if we are excluded from the good freedom": Thwarted Expectations of Independence in the Luapula Province of Zambia, 1964-1966," *Journal of African History* 47 (2006).

11 For an interesting recent analysis of genesis of authoritarianism within UNIP, see Giacomo Macola, "Harry Mwaanga Nkumbula, UNIP and the roots of authoritarianism in nationalist Zambia," in Gewald, Hinfelaar and Macola (eds.), *One Zambia*, pp. 17- 44.

12 See Miles Larmer, "Enemies within?: Opposition to the Zambia one-party state, 1972-1980," in Gewald, Hinfelaar and Macola (eds.), *One Zambia*, p. 103.

newspapers reports that allude to the chief's views after the 1970s perhaps reflect the authors' own views, rather than those of the potentate himself. Unavoidably, this chapter is based on these frustratingly fragmentary sources. It is vital to bear this in mind when reading this chapter.

It is within the context of Zambia's deepening social, economic, and political crises outlined above that one may have at least a glimpse of the transformations that took place in the Chewa Paramount Chief's perspectives between the early 1970s and 2004. To be sure, Kalonga Gawa Undi X continued to be an active supporter of the UNIP government well up to the late 1980s. Nonetheless, he came to link the decline in rural agriculture and its attendant worsening poverty to the regime's inefficiency and corruption. The traditional ruler, therefore, linked hands with other traditional rulers in eastern Zambia such as Chiefs Sayiri, Nyanje, and Mkanda, who from the 1970s onward became bitter critics of inefficiency, incompetence, and corruption in high corridors of power.

Chief Sayiri perhaps most eloquently articulated the growing discontent among these rulers engendered by the debilitating incompetence of the UNIP government and particularly its failure to boost agricultural production in the countryside. Addressing the Rural District Council in Chipata at a meeting attended by both President Kenneth Kaunda and Kalonga Gawa Undi X early in the 1970s, Sayiri particularly singled out government-appointed functionaries for a scathing attack. Referring specifically to agricultural extension officers, he attributed falling agricultural production to government officials. The irate Chief noted that these officials were "not working as hard [as] they used to work during the colonial days," and he castigated their poor knowledge of farming as the root cause of the falling agricultural output in Zambia.

These sentiments were echoed by Chiefs Mkanda, Nyanje and Kalonga Gawa Undi X. Despite President Kaunda's presence at the meeting, the chiefs collectively attributed falling agricultural production to his government's failure to deliver agro-inputs on time and to collect harvested crops before the rains commenced. Even more pointedly, they argued that agricultural technocrats in the province were unable to carry out their duties efficiently because of too much political interference by the ruling party. To eradicate this problem, these traditional rulers challenged the President and his government to grant more power to technocrats in productivity committees in the province than to UNIP politicians.[13] Much to

---

[13] NAZ EP 4/1/106, Minutes of the chiefs' meeting held in the Rural Chambers on 16 January 1970

the surprise of Kaunda, they also blamed the plight of rural Zambians on his government's indifference to the welfare of rural dwellers. Such criticism is all the more remarkable as the President himself usually exonerated his party and government from the growing economic woes in the country. In contrast to traditional authorities, he portrayed the falling levels of food production in rural areas as a consequence of the villagers' own unwillingness to work hard and of their chiefs' indifference to his economic policies.[14]

In condemning government incompetence, the Chewa leader added his voice to popular opposition to the UNIP regime long before the founding of the Movement for Multi-party Democracy (MMD) in the late 1980s, which successfully de-campaigned UNIP from office in 1991.[15] Yet despite his condemnation, Gawa Undi X continued to support the government publicly, until at least the late 1980s. Until then, he endorsed its economic reforms.[16] In the same vein, the Chewa sovereign actively supported President Kenneth Kaunda's foreign policy through which the latter uncompromisingly committed Zambia to the struggle for political freedom in southern African territories still ruled by white minority regimes.

The identification by the Paramount Chief of the incompetence of the post-colonial regime with economic malaise may ironically elucidate why he embraced its self-help economic reforms aimed at combating escalating rural poverty between the 1970s and 1980s. Like UNIP officials, Kalonga Gawa Undi X seems to have come to believe that the Zambian government alone could not eradicate poverty. He, therefore, turned into an active advocate of government-sponsored self-help schemes, notably producer, consumer and marketing cooperatives. From the late 1970s, he reportedly tirelessly urged his subordinate chiefs with their followers to form cooperatives as a means to combat poverty. To this end, the traditional ruler frequently toured his chiefdoms to hold meetings at which he spelt out the advantages of forming cooperatives. According to an eyewitness, he meticulously planned each of such meetings in advance to attract as many attendees as possible. About a week or so before holding a meeting in a particular village, the Paramount Chief, the informant recalled, notified its headmen or chief about the meeting.[17] This enabled the subordinate chief

---

at 8.50 A.M.

[14] Ibid.

[15] After several decades of scholarly neglect, there is now a small but growing body of literature that deals with unpopular opposition to the UNIP-led government between 1964 and 1991. See for example, Macola, "Thwarted expectations of independence"; Macola, "Harry Mwaanga Nkumbula" and David M. Gordon, "Rebellion or massacre?: The UNIP-Lumpa conflict revisited," in Gewald, Hinfelaar and Macola (eds.), *One Zambia*, pp. 45-76.

[16] For details on these reforms, see Macmillan, "Mulungushi Reforms".

or headman to inform as many followers as possible about the pending meeting.

Unsurprisingly, the meetings at which the Paramount Chief urged his subjects to create cooperatives were often well attended. To stimulate public interest in cooperatives, Kalonga Gawa Undi X turned these gatherings into an occasion for officially handing over to cooperative members agricultural in-puts, such as fertilisers, seeds, and ploughs. In this way, the potentate, who reportedly was also well-versed in Zambia's post-colonial economic rhetoric that placed a premium on economic self-reliance and diligence, successfully drummed up mass support for the cooperative movement. Speaking in idioms that were locally familiar, he evidently persuaded many of his followers to join one form of cooperative society or another. As some of his subjects recalled recently, the traditional ruler

Photo 5 Kalonga Gawa Undi X handing over a plough to a member of a Cooperative Society. Courtesy of National Archives of Zambia

---

[17] Interview with Alick Chafunya Phiri, Headman, Kafumbwe village, 08 August 2008.

hoped that this would enable people to not only effectively mobilise more agricultural inputs such as fertilizers, labour, and equipment but also gain easier access to credit and markets.[18]

But cooperatives proved to be a poor panacea to Zambia's economic doldrums. Like other sectors of the post-colonial economy such as retail trade which the Kaunda regime wanted to be monopolised by indigenous Zambians rather than expatriate businessmen, the cooperative movement scarcely escaped from a host of debilitating impediments.[19] These ranged from poor rural communication infrastructure and non-availability of credit to rampant financial embezzlements, employment of unqualified managers and inefficiency.[20] As a corollary, by the 1980s, most of the cooperatives in the country as a whole were as good as dead. This notwithstanding, it is indisputable that in Chewa-speaking areas, Kalonga Gawa Undi X had been the moving spirit behind the creation of most of the cooperatives.[21] His subjects unsurprisingly credited him with having inspired the formation of more cooperatives in his areas than any other chief in the Eastern province as a whole.[22]

Whether these celebratory reminiscences are accurate or not, the strenuous efforts the Paramount Chief put in establishing cooperative societies in areas under his control plainly demonstrate his commitment to engage his subjects in self-help economic ventures to fight escalating poverty. The traditional ruler perceived these schemes as a short step to reducing his followers' dependence on handouts from the government, whose inability to improve the living standard of the people was glaring by the late 1970s. Understood from this perspective, the support that Kalonga Gawa Undi X rendered to the cooperative movement reflects his realisation that the UNIP government alone with its incompetence, corruption, and inefficiency would never make good its pre-independence promise of a better life for all. Nor could it meet the social and political expectations of the majority of Zambians. The people, the Paramount Chief repeatedly told his followers, had to help themselves through their own initiative, resourcefulness, and hard work.[23]

---

[18] Interview with Alick Chafunya Phiri, Headman, Kafumbwe Sub-Centre, 08 August 2008; Peter Chaima Phiri, former migrant worker, Mnthipa village, 07 August 2008.
[19] See Macmillan, "Mulungushi Reforms," pp. 209-210.
[20] Personal communication with Reuben Phiri.
[21] Interviews with Kamlendo Phiri, Headman, Mnthipa Village, 07 August 2008; Alick Chafunya Phiri, Kafumbwe Sub-Centre, 08 August 2008.
[22] Ibid.
[23] Alick Chafunya Phiri, interview cited.

Gawa Undi X in the Liberation of Mozambique

If Kalonga Gawa Undi X came to doubt the ability of the post-colonial regime in Zambia to deal with growing economic woes in the country from the 1970s onward, he, nonetheless, unstintingly supported its foreign policy in relation to the liberation of colonies still controlled by white minority regimes in southern Africa.[24] It is very tempting to think that the attitude of the Paramount Chief to the politics of decolonisation in the region was moulded by government rhetoric that equated the liberation of neighbouring colonies with Zambia's own political and economic survival. With the benefit of hindsight, however, there seem to have been deep ethno-historical dynamics that propelled the Chewa sovereign to support the nationalist struggle in southern Africa generally, and in nearby Mozambique particularly. The role the chief played in the liberation of Mozambique cannot hence be fully comprehended outside the context of these dynamics. It is to this topic that we now turn.

As shown in Chapter 1, the Chewa people over whom Gawa Undi X reigned in Zambia are descendants of immigrants whose remote origins can be traced to the present-day Katanga province in the Democratic Republic of Congo and their more immediate origins in Mozambique.[25] There is consensus among students of east-central Africa history that the immigrants first settled in Malawi, where they established the Kalonga kingdom around or before the 16th century. The kingdom, which may have

---

[24] The body of literature on Zambia's role in the liberation of the sub-region is legion. For studies that explore the topic from a macro perspective, see Benedict V. Mtshali, "Zambia's Foreign Policy: The Dilemma of a New State," (unpublished doctoral dissertation, New York University, 1972); Richard L. Sklar, "Zambia's response to the Rhodesian declaration of independence," in William Tordoff (ed.), *Politics in Zambia* (Manchester: Manchester University Press, 1974); Dastun W. Kamana, "Zambia," in Douglas G. Anglin, Timothy M. Shawa and Carl G. Widstrand (eds.), *Conflict and Change in Southern Africa: Papers from a Scandinavian-Canadian Conference* (Washington DC.: University Press of America, 1978), pp. 33-68; Douglas G. Anglin and Timothy M. Shawa, *Zambia's Foreign Policy: Studies in Diplomacy and Development* (Colorado: Westview Press, 1979); Mukelebai Songiso, "Zambia's Role in Southern Africa," MA dissertation, 1989. More recent studies that share the same perspective are Andrew J. Deroche, "'You can't fight guns with knives': National security and Zambian responses to UDI, 1965-1975," in Gewald, Hinfelaar and Macola (eds.), *One Zambia*, pp. 76-97; Clarence Choongo, "The Impact of the Liberation Struggles on Zambia with Special Reference to the Unilateral Declaration of Independence," MA dissertation, University of Zambia, forthcoming; Alexander Grey Zulu, *Memoirs of Alexander Grey Zulu* (Ndola: Printpak, 2007). For a recent study that adopts a micro view of Zambia's involvement in the liberation wars in southern Africa after the country's independence in 1964, see Walima T. Kalusa, "Eastern Zambia in the Liberation of Mozambique," "Lusaka: Manuscript, SADC Hashim Mbita Project 2008).

[25] For a sophisticated analysis of the rise, expansion, and fall of the Chewa empire, see Harry Wells Langworthy III, "A History of Undi's Kingdom to 1890: Aspects of Chewa History in East Central Africa," (unpublished doctoral dissertation, Boston University, 1969). For an amateur interpretation of the creation of the Chewa kingdom, see Listard Elifala Banda, *The Chewa Kingdom* (Lusaka: Desert Enterprise Limited, 2002. The material in this and the next three paragraphs derives largely from Kalusa, "Eastern Zambia,"

extended as far as pre-colonial Zambia, seems to have been plagued by social and political tensions. This compelled disaffected factions within the ruling elite to migrate elsewhere in search of their own polities. One of such factions was led by Gawa Undi, who before the 16th century founded his own polity headquartered at Mano in what is now the Tete province of Mozambique.[26]

The successors of the founder of the Chewa kingdom in Mozambique did not relocate to modern Zambia until as late as the 1930s. Nonetheless, long before the relocation, their military power and influence apparently extended to non-Chewa speaking people. These included the Nsenga, the Bisa, Senga and other people in both present-day Zambia and Malawi. Indeed, it seems that Kalonga Gawa Undi's influence over time overshadowed that of Kalonga in the latter territory. In this way, the subjects of Kalonga Gawa Undi in Mozambique forged lasting political, economic, and socio-cultural bonds with their counterparts in pre-colonial Malawi and Zambia. Indeed, his subjects in all the three territories areas periodically forwarded tribute to Mano in return for the king's protection and spiritual blessings. Such ties were reinforced from 1935 or 1936 onwards when the reigning Kalonga Gawa Undi relocated his capital village to Katete in Northern Rhodesia.[27] This move was perhaps made to escape the more draconian rule of the Portuguese colonial administration in Mozambique.[28] Long after the relocation, his subjects in Mozambique, Zambia and Malawi continued to recognise him and his successors as their overlords, sending them tribute in kind in return of which they received spiritual and economic blessings from Undi. As demonstrated in the final chapter of this study, this practice continues to be enacted at the annual Kulamba ceremony in Katete that brings together thousands of Chewa-speaking people from within Zambia, Malawi and Mozambique.

This abbreviated account of the rise of the Chewa kingdom is indicative of the fact that in spite of the balkanisation of the Chewa kingdom between the British and the Portuguese in the 19th century, the Chewa nation survived albeit in an emasculated form. As would be expected, social ties involving the Chewa and Nsenga in the three colonies were continually oiled through intermarriages and other social alliances. This situation both

---

26 Langworthy III, "History of Undi's Kingdom".
27 Zulu, *Memoirs*, p. 389.
28 On the brutality of Portuguese rule in Mozambique, see Richard Gibson, *African Liberation Movements: Contemporary Struggles against White Minority Rule* (London, Oxford, and New York: Oxford University Press, 1972), p. 272-275

predated and outlived colonialism.[29] Imperial rule, therefore, did little to undermine pre-existing political, linguistic and socio-cultural interconnections between eastern Zambia and Mozambique. To the contrary, Portuguese colonialism in particular contributed to cementing these links. Africans, who fled from the draconian and repressive rule of the Portuguese administration in Mozambique, frequently sought sanctuary in eastern Zambia. An example will suffice. In 1917, about 100,000 Mozambicans fled into neighbouring eastern Zambia, Malawi, and Zimbabwe to escape the brutality of Portuguese authorities as they tried to quell an African rebellion against the exploitation of concession companies.[30] In Zambia's Eastern province, they settled mostly in Chewa districts.

It is reasonable to suggest that the deep ethnic and historical ties between the local people in eastern Zambia and Mozambicans predisposed Kalonga Gawa Undi X together with his subordinate chiefs and their subjects to welcome Mozambican exiles and freedom fighters once the liberation struggle intensified in Mozambique in the late 1960s and 1970s. This enabled the Chewa ruling elite to augment their own social standing and political following with additional subjects whose historical, ethnic, cultural, and linguistic background was synonymous with that of the local people.[31]

With tacit or active encouragement from the Paramount Chief, Mozambican refugees unsurprisingly came to form a substantial proportion of the population in Chewa-speaking areas. After the Liberation Front of Mozambique (FRELIMO) opened its second front in Mozambique's Tete province close to Chadiza in Zambia in 1968, the number of Mozambican refugees turned into a deluge. By 1974 as the independence war in Mozambique neared its end, there were thousands of Mozambican runaways in Eastern province as a whole. There, the majority of the exiles ensconced themselves in chiefdoms under Gawa Undi X, whose subjects fed and sheltered the exiles.[32]

The support that the Chewa of Zambia extended to exiles and to the nationalist war effort in the neighbouring colony drew upon their heads the wrath of Portuguese military forces in Mozambique in the 1970s. In the

---

[29] Interview with Lyson Chigaga Phiri, Headman/Senior Advisor to Paramount Chief Gawa Undi, Mwanzaulungu Village, Katete, 11 September 2007.
[30] Andrew Kombe Zulu, "Mozambican Refugees at Ukwimi Agricultural Settlement: The Socio-Economi Contributions to Petauke District, 1987-1993," BA Undergraduate Research Paper, University of Zambia, 1996," p. 3.
[31] Lyson Chigaga Phiri, interview cited.
[32] Ibid.

following decade, it also provoked retaliatory military actions from of the Mozambique Resistance Army (MNR), infamously known as RENAMO. Both Portuguese and RENAMO incursions in areas under the Paramount Chief cannot be abstracted from the wider policy of destabilisation pursued by white minority regimes in southern Africa from 1970 to the late 1980s.[33] Needless to say, the principal goal of this policy was to undermine the military power of liberation movements against white-controlled regimes, as well as Zambia's political stability and economy. This was in an endeavour to compel the Zambian government to jettison its southern African liberation agenda. Portuguese military strategists and authorities in Mozambique hoped to fulfil these objectives by destroying settlements in Zambia that played host to refugees and freedom fighters and by sabotaging the country's bridges, railways and other economic infrastructure.

The influx of Mozambican refugees into and the close identification of the chiefdoms under Kalonga Gawa Undi X with Mozambican guerrilla activities against Portuguese colonial forces turned Chewa chiefdoms into a prized target of the Portuguese policy of destabilisation. From the early 1970s onward, border villages in particularly Katete and Chadiza, which harboured thousands of Mozambican refugees and which colonial authorities in Mozambique often accused of shielding *bandidos armados* (armed bandits), as the Portuguese contemptuously branded FRELIMO freedom fighters, became objects of regular raids. In 1972, for example, the Portuguese army and warplanes bombarded and completely destroyed Walilanya village on the Chadiza-Tete border. In the melee, enemy troops killed undisclosed number of Zambian villagers. They also reportedly raped women, bayoneted children, torched houses and stole livestock.[34] Other border settlements that suffered a similar fate were Lote and Vubwi in Chadiza, Kafumbwe, Chikabala, Kanthumba and Chilawe in Katete and in Nyanje in Petauke, where Portuguese troops drove Chief Mwanjabanthu out from his palace and occupied it for a brief period in the 1970s.[35] Hundreds of people were uprooted from their villages, with most of them relocating away from the border areas to seek sanctuary in the interior of Chadiza, Katete, Nyimba, Petauke, and even Chipata, the provincial capital of Eastern province. New villages such as the one at Tefelansoni in Chadiza today were founded by refugees fleeing from villages on the Zambia-Mo-

---

[33] See Zulu, *Memoirs*. Most of the material in this section emanates from Kalusa, "Eastern Zambia".
[34] Anelo Makowa Mwale, interview cited.
[35] Ferdinand M. Banda, Politician/Induna, Petauke Stores, Petauke, 14 September 2007.

zambique frontier.[36]

The assistance that Kalonga Gawa Undi X and his chiefs proffered to the war effort in Mozambique came to haunt them, too, a few years after that country's independence in 1975. From 1987 to 1989, Chewa villages were not infrequently terrorised by RENAMO.[37] Briefly, RENAMO, a brainchild of the white-dominated regimes in South Africa and in Southern Rhodesia, emerged in the late 1970s principally to destabilise the FRELIMO-controlled government in Mozambique. Armed and sponsored by the South African racist regime after the fall of Ian Smith's minority government in 1980, RENAMO plunged Mozambique into a long and bitter civil war from 1987 onwards. As Chewa-speaking areas under the Paramount Chief supported the FRELIMO both before and after Mozambican independence, RENAMO rebels began to carry out cross-border reprisals into eastern Zambia, its first recorded incursion there taking place in March 1987.[38]

This raid marked the beginning of RENAMO incursions into the province. RENAMO reprisals took the form of pillaging, cattle rustling, abductions, mutilations and arson. The most horrifying of these actions perhaps occurred on December 20, 1987 when RENAMO rebels armed with axes, spears, machine guns and rocket launchers attacked and overran an immigration post and a cooperative shop in Chadiza on the Zambia-Mozambique border. They abducted eight people, looted houses, torched a vehicle and stole money along with nearly 300 heads of cattle. Close to a corpse of one of their victims, the rebels left a letter warning the Zambian government that such actions would persist unless the country refrained from supporting the FRELIMO-dominated government in Mozambique.[39]

This was not an empty warning. RENAMO cross-border incursions into Zambia's Eastern province as a whole intensified between 1987 and 1989. Collectively, these raids claimed seventy-five lives in that period. They further resulted in the abduction of a total of forty-one Zambians, the stealing of hundreds of heads of cattle and the destruction of more than 170 houses and twenty-eight shops.[40] The most harrowing method of killing by RENAMO rebels is still remembered with terror among the Chewa in-

---

36 Alifasi Kafumu Banda, interview cited; Anelo Makowa Mwale, interview cited.
37 For a detailed study on RENAMO organisation, see Alex Vine, *RENAMO: Terrorism in Mozambique* (University of York: Centre for African Studies; London: James Currey, and Bloomington and Indianapolis, 1991).
38 Vine, *RENAMO*, p. 65; see also Zulu, Memoirs, pp. 339-340.
39 Ibid.
40 Zulu, *Memoirs*, pp. 339-340.

volved pounding babies in a mortar with pestle or bayoneting them as their hapless and distraught Zambian mothers looked on.[41]

Questioning Government Credentials

The impunity and regularity with which Portuguese forces and RENA-MO bandits terrorised eastern Zambia coupled with falling standards of living after 1973 demonstrated the Zambian government's inability to protect its citizens from either external enemies or poverty. In this situation, all Kalonga Gawa Undi X could do was to fly by a helicopter, which was supplied by the Zambian government, to villages that had been raided to offer his personal consolations to the victims of Portuguese incursions.[42] The failure of the government to protect people from external aggression, rising poverty, and UNIP's expanding authoritarianism provided the context that shaped the Chief's attitude towards the call for the return to multi-party politics in the late 1980s. To be sure, the evidence that links the protagonist to the Movement of Multi-party Democracy (MMD) that championed the crusade for the restoration of multi-party politics towards the end of the 1980s is more circumstantial than concrete. What part the Chief played in the campaign, therefore, remains somewhat blurred.

However, eyewitnesses in the Eastern province recall that Frederick Jacob Chiluba, the President of MMD and other top officials in the movement, became regular visitors at the Paramount Chief's palace at Mkaika in Katete, as they vigorously campaigned to win over the backing of traditional rulers across the country in order to dismantle UNIP's hold on power.[43] The regularity with which the proponents of pro-democracy politics courted Kalonga Gawa Undi X implies that the latter did at least tacitly welcome the abolition of the despotic rule of the UNIP regime. This is notwithstanding the fact that the MMD failed to dislodge UNIP from areas under the Chewa ruler in the 1991 elections through which Chiluba overwhelmingly defeated Kaunda and the MMD booted UNIP out of office.

If the potentate and other people had hoped that the new government under President Frederick Chiluba would find the magic stick with which they could deliver to Zambians the proverbial golden egg, they were soon to be disillusioned. Eager to become what Jeremy Gould aptly describes as "model pupils of structural adjustment," Chiluba and his cabinet swallowed hook and sink the so-called free market policies formulated by financial

---

41 Interview with Hilario Kasumba, Chadiza Basic School, Chadiza, 10 September 2007.
42 Interview with Kafuwa Yobe Chimbelekero, Headman, Kafumbwe, 08 August 2008.
43 James Nyirongo and Mama Nyangu, interviews cited

lending institutions led by the International Monetary Fund and the World Bank. To this end, they not only hurriedly sold off the country's public assets, including mines.[44] They also, inter alia, threw to the winds regulations on the value of the country's currency, abolished restrictions on both exports and imports, removed government subsidies from peasant commodity producers, and introduced user-fees in public schools and hospitals.

The ultimate outcome of these reforms was catastrophic. Rather than mend the economic damage the previous regime had left behind, they worsened it. Under free market policies, which President Chiluba surprisingly eloquently defended, thousands of Zambians were retrenched, as industries folded up one after another.[45] By 1994, only 11 per cent of the country's labour force of not less than four million people were employed.[46] This state of affairs was exacerbated by rising crime, the crippling HIV/AIDS pandemic, escalating corruption and deepening rural poverty.

It is against this backcloth that one may best appreciate why before his death in 2004 the sovereign became a staunch supporter of President Levy Patrick Mwanawasa, who on assuming office from Chiluba in 2001 launched a nationwide crusade against poverty, corruption and HIV/AIDS. When the new President sacked his deputy information minister for corruption and threatened to fire several other ministers suspected of the same vice in 2003, for example, the traditional leader lauded Mwanawasa's tough anti-corruption stand as "the right thing to do".[47] Likewise, he supported the President's efforts to revive the agricultural sector in the expectation that this development would "bring about positive change in the country".[48]

But the enthusiastic response of the former freedom fighter to the policies of President Levy Patrick Mwanawasa came with strings. In 2003, Kalonga Gawa Undi X challenged the new President to re-surface the Great East Road in order to speed up economic development in the Eastern province. More importantly, aware of the erosion of the power and authority traditional leaders had suffered at the hands of the previous regimes, he futher urged President Mwanawasa to revive the House of Chiefs. At a meeting with the President on 12 April 2003, the irrepressible ruler won-

---

[44] Jeremy Gould, "Subsidiary sovereignty and the constitution of political space in Zambia," in Gewald, Hinfelaar and Macola (eds.), *One Zambia*, p. 279.

[45] *Times of Zambia*, 31 August 1994.

[46] Friday E. Mulenga, "Fighting for democracy of the pocket: The labour movement of the Third Republic," in Gewald, Hinfelaar and Macola (eds), *One Zambia*, pp. 243-258.

[47] *Sunday Times of Zambia*, 13 April 2003.

[48] Ibid.

dered why the House had been dormant for more than ten years despite its having been enshrined in the independence constitution in whose construction Kalonga Gawa Undi X himself actively took part in London many decades earlier.[49]

His request for the resuscitation of the House of Chiefs fell on President Mwanawasa's receptive ears. A few months after the meeting, his government put aside K753 million for the resumption of the meetings of the House of Chief in an effort to bring traditional authorities closer to the government.[50] But Kalonga Gawa Undi X did not live long enough to see the revival of the House of Chiefs. Early in August 2003, he was hospitalised for meningitis at St Francis hospital in Katete district, and was later moved to the University Teaching Hospital, Lusaka, for further treatment.[51] The Paramount Chief never fully recovered from the affliction. On 21 November 2004, at the age seventy-three, he passed away at Mkaika palace, Katete. A week later on 2 December 2004, the Chewa Royal Establishment installed his grand-nephew Fred Daka as his successor.[52] The following day, the deceased Paramount Chief, nationalist, and agent of modernity was interred at his final resting at Dole in Katete.

Conclusion

This chapter has attempted to chronicle shifts in the political and economic perspectives of Kalonga Gawa Undi X in the decades that preceded his death in 2004. Placing the discussion within the broader context of the economic, social and political doldrums that plagued Zambia from the 1970s onward, the chapter asserts that the Chewa ruler continued to be an ally of the Kaunda government well up to the late 1980s. For most of the time, he unquestionably endorsed its economic and political policies. Over time, however, Kalonga Gawa Undi X grew increasingly apprehensive over the government's failure to tackle a wide range of problems: rising poverty, corruption, political intolerance,and the erosion of the power and influence of traditional leaders. It is for this reason that the Chief lent his support to the call for a return to multi-party politics by the MMD towards the end of the 1980s and early 1990s. He, for the same reason, supported President Levy Mwanawasa in his war against corruption, and he successfully lobbied the government to re-open the House of Chiefs in 2003. In this

---

49 Ibid.
50 *Sunday Times of Zambia*, 25 May 2003.
51 *Times of Zambia*, 1 August 2003.
52 *Times of Zambia*, 2 December 2004.

way, the veteran politician hoped to restore to his fellow traditional rulers their lost authority, their status, their prerogatives and, above all, their voice in running the affairs of the country.

6

The Quest for Regional Integration

Introduction

Two decades prior to his death in 2004, Kalonga Gawa Undi X revived the Kulamba ceremony of the Chewa-speaking people in Zambia, Malawi and Mozambique. It is surprising that the Paramount Chief resuscitated this cultural event after it had been in abeyance since 1934, when it was banned by colonial authorities at the instigation of European missionaries. To missionaries, the ceremony, like other non-Christian traditional forms with their associated dances and rituals, was a primordial and "pagan" affair that stood in the path of African conversion to Christianity. It is astonishing that by the time Kalonga Gawa Undi X revived the ceremony, the Paramount Chief himself had been an adherent to Christianity for over many decades, and he never recanted the faith. Why, then, did he resuscitate the Kulamba ceremony? How did he reconcile his Christianity with the ceremony, whose rituals and dances notably the Gule Wamkulu (Nyau) dance were regarded by missionaries as no more than an obstacle that marred African belief in the Christian ideology? What transformations have taken place in the ceremony since its revival in 1984? And, finally, what has been its significance to the Chewa people, to Zambia and to the southern African region as a whole since its restoration?

This chapter seeks to address these queries in an endeavour to comprehend why the Christian Paramount Chief restored the "pagan" Kulamba ceremony, and it examines the changes that have occurred in this cultural event since its revival. The chapter suggests that in resuscitating the Kulamba cultural ceremony, Kalonga Gawa Undi X hoped to accomplish both cultural and geo-political goals. Notwithstanding his devotion to the Christian ideology, the potentate perceived Kulamba ceremony as the surest path to reinvigorating African culture. Similarly, he saw it as a unifying force that would not only unite the Chewa people within his chiefdoms alone. Kalonga Gawa Undi X evidently believed that the ceremony could strengthen the ties and cooperation between the ten million Chewa speakers who live in Malawi, Zambia and Mozambique and between them and non-Chewa people alike in southern Africa as a whole.

It is also apparent that the Paramount Ruler envisaged that cooperation and unity spawned by Kulamba would foster economic and political development in the region. To Kalonga Gawa Undi X, therefore, the ceremony was not merely a viable instrument of cultural preservation. It was also a vehicle of social, economic and regional integration, a condition that he saw as a prerequisite to peace, economic stability, and prosperity in Zambia and beyond. In pursuing cultural preservation, regional integration and economic prosperity through the Kulamba ceremony, the traditional ruler won the accolades of political authorities in Zambia particularly and in the region generally. This issued from their appreciation of the vital role the Kulamba ceremony could play as regards boosting tourism, economic development, and political goodwill within and between countries in southern Africa.[1]

Literature Review

There is a paucity of information on Zambia's traditional ceremonies in general and on the Kulamba ceremony in particular. This partly issues from sheer lack of interest among historians and other scholars in traditional ceremonies, but perhaps more importantly, partly from the scarcity of primary evidence on cultural events. A large part of data for this chapter thus largely derives from oral sources. Admittedly there are a few studies on Chewa history. Disappointingly, most of these works do not treat Kulamba as an integral aspect of Chewa history and culture.[2] Moreover, they are inaccessible to English-speakers as they are written in ChiChewa. Among such studies include those by Jonas Makumbi and E.B. Mwale.[3] Makumbi provides a rich description of Chewa traditions, particularly the rituals associated with funeral rites. However, Makumba makes only a passing reference to the Kulamba traditional ceremony.

[1] See Levy Patrick Mwanawasa, "Speech by His Excellency the President of the Republic of Zambia, Mr Levy Patrick Mwanawasa, SC, on the Occasion of the 2007 Kulamba Traditional Ceremony of the Chewa of Malawi, Mozambique and Zambia on the 25th August, 2007 at Mkaika Palace in Katete."

[2] See, for example, H.W. Langworthy, "A History of Undi's Kingdom to 1890: Aspects of Chewa History in East Central Africa," PhD dissertation: Boston University, 1969.

[3] Jonas A. Makumbi, *Maliro Ndi Miyambo Ya Achewa* (Blantyre: Dzuka Publishing Company, Ltd, 1965 and E.B Mwale, *Za Achewa* (Lusaka: Macmillan, 1982).

On the other hand, E.B. Mwale's monograph illustrates the general history of the Chewa people. Among other things, this study chronicles their movements, their areas of settlement, and their cultural practices. In addition, it highlights the different kinds of tribute that the Chewa historically forwarded to successive Chewa overlords in recognition of their power or authority.[4] As it is practised today, the core of the Kulamba ceremony inheres in paying tribute to the Paramount Chief by his subjects from Zambia, Malawi and Mozambique. As in the past, tribute payment reinforces the political power, prestige and authority of the Chewa ruler.

In recent days, academic analysts including Ian and Jane Linden have recognised the critical role indigenous African institutions have historically played in power politics at grassroots level.[5] They have demonstrated that the Nyau society, an ancient Chewa institution, for example, engaged in politics of exclusion to contest Catholic missionary teachings in nineteenth- and twentieth-century Nyasaland (now Malawi). In this way, the Lindens argue, Nyau adherents minimised the impact of Christianity on their cultural life at village level in the central region of Malawi.[6] From this perspective, the Nyau brotherhood in colonial Malawi, and presumably Zambia, was part and parcel of the anti-colonial protest. It is no surprise, then, that the institution was anathema to the spread of the Christian ideology, and therefore quickly aroused the wrath of Christian missionaries.

The hostility between Nyau societies and Western evangelists in central Africa symbolised the clash between indigenous traditional culture and the so-called Western civilisation. This conflict was magnified partly by the fact that European missionaries seldom comprehended African culture and partly by their belief that there would be no cultural exchange between them and the people they encountered in Africa. Indeed, missionaries seldom paid attention to the functions local institutions played in the African society. In their view, Nyau societies with their esoteric dances and rituals were little more than pagan, archaic relics of primitive societies irreconcilably anathema to Western civilisation, Christianity and modernity. To Christian missionaries, as Linden and Linden argue:

---

[4] Mwale, *Za Achewa*, Chapter six. See also p. 30.

[5] See for instance Ian Linden, "Chewa Initiation Rites and Nyau Societies: The Use of Religious Institutions in Local Politics at Mua," in T.O. Ranger and John Weller (eds.) *Themes in the Christian History of Central Africa*, (Lusaka: Heinemann, 1975), pp.30-45.,and Matthew Schoffellers and Ian Linden, "The Resistance of the Nyau Societies to the Roman Catholic Missions in Colonial Malawi," in T. O. Ranger and I. N. Kimambo (eds.) *The Historical Study of African Religion with Special Reference to East and Central Africa*. (Nairobi: Heinemann, 1972), pp,252-271.

[6] Ian Linden and Jane Linden, *Catholics, Peasants and Chewa Resistance in Nyasaland, 1889-1939* (London: Heinemann, 1974), p. 117.

The nyau was immoral ... because of the sexual content of the songs, the appearance of naked dancers in the presence of women, and because [missionaries] had reason to believe that there were instances of adultery taking place after the performances.[7]

Christian missionaries held that African traditional culture, as manifested in Nyau dances and rituals, was a high barrier they had to cross to plant the seed of their faith in the "Dark Continent". It is from this standpoint that Nyau societies became a major target of missionary onslaught. But, Nyau societies themselves took counteractive measures against Christian evangelism. As the Lindens show, they turned into more or less a political institution that contested Christian cultural hegemony in an effort to shield their own culture from Christian contamination.[8]

Another study that as much relates popular culture to political resistance in British Africa as it explores the interconnection between African dance forms to social and economic change is Albert Matongo's work on Mbeni and Kalela dances on the Zambian Copperbelt.[9] Matongo insists that both Kalela and Mbeni dances not only played an instrumental role in sensitising the urban population to the injustices of colonial rule. They also, he argues, developed as an effective medium of nationalist agitation against imperial control.[10]

In view of the foregoing arguments, it is reasonable to stress that cultural forms such as Kalela, Mbeni, and Nyau are not just a traditional means of entertainment. These popular dances have historically been deployed to champion the social, economic and political welfare by people in societies far removed in time and space. As Matongo shows, Kalela on the Copperbelt in the 20th century particularly served as a means by which African nationalist parties mobilised mass following against colonial subjugation and oppression.

Put in other words, cultural forms, including the Kulamba ceremony, have historically undergone permutations in terms of the uses to which their performers have put them. They are, therefore, seldom conservative forces, although they are often perceived in such terms. As the discussion

---

[7] Linden and Linden, *Catholics, Peasants and Chewa Resistance*, p. 119.
[8] Linden and Linden, *Catholics, Peasants and Chewa Resistance*.
[9] Albert B.K. Matongo, 'Popular Culture in a Colonial Society: Another Look at Mbeni and Kalela Dance on the Copperbelt, 1930-1964' in Samuel Chipungu (ed.) *Guardians in Their Time: Experiences of Zambians Under Colonial Rule, 1890-1964* (London: Macmillan, 1992), pp.180-210. For a detailed study on Kalela alone, see J. Clyde Mitchell, "The Kalela Dance: Aspects of Social Relationships among Urban Africans in Northern Rhodesia," *Rhodes-Livingstone Papers* 27 (Manchester: Manchester University Press, 1956).
[10] Matongo, 'Popular Culture in a Colonial Society', p. 208.

on Kulamba below suggests, traditional ceremonies acquire new functions in shifting historical and political constellations. As a sequel, they have been employed in societies removed in time and space to bring about desirable change, even though they are sometimes deployed to preserve some aspects of their actors' culture.[11]

Genesis of Kulamba Ceremony: A Historical Interpretation.

The history of this ceremony is synonymous with the history of the Chewa-speaking people. As noted earlier in this study, the Chewa were one of the groups of Bantu people whose remote origins may be traced to the modern day Democratic Republic of the Congo, and their more recent origins to present-day Mozambique.[12] They are part of a group of people commonly referred to as Bantu, who carried with them Luba-Lunda chiefly and other political symbols and introduced them in central southern Africa. Like other Bantu ethnic groups, the Chewa are also credited with having evolved cultural ideologies and practices that defined their socio-political culture and life.

There is unanimity in oral sources that the Kulamba ceremony was the product of the cultural entrepreneurship of the Phiri clan that came to prominence as the Chewa (or Maravi) migrated from the present-day Democratic Republic of Congo to modern Malawi in or before the 15 century.[13] According to Chewa court historians, the Phiri clan clan initiated the Kulamba ceremony as a way of ensuring the loyalty of subordinate chiefs to whom Kalonga dispensed the land he conquered en route to Malawi. Legend has it that upon vanquishing a territory, Kalonga installed and left behind a sub-chief to 'look after' that particular area, while the overlord himself proceeded to conquer other territories. Junior chiefs to whom the king awarded land and political titles were invariably expected to return the favour.

According to Chewa royal discourse, Kalonga's subordinate rulers individually and at different times brought tribute to him in form of slaves,

---

11 This point is made most poignantly by Mapopa Mtonga, "The Drama of Gule Wamkulu: A Study of the Nyau as Practised by the Chewa of Eastern Province of Zambia," M.A. Thesis, University of Ghana, institute of African Studies, Legon, 1980). See also M. Chinyanta and C.J. Chiwale, *Mutomboko Ceremony and Kazembe Dynasty*, (Lusaka: Kenneth Kaunda Foundation, 1989).

12 Banda, *The Chewa Kingdom*, p. 12. The history of the Chewa people has been discussed in considerable detail elsewhere in this book.

13 Interview with Lameck Daka, Headman, Chilembwe Village, Katete, Zambia, 9th August, 2008., interview with G. Chigwala, Headman, Chigwala Village, Katete, Zambia, 9th August, 2008., interview with Headman Yobe Kafuwa Chimbelekelo, Kafumbwe Basic School, Katete, Zambia, 8th August, 2008; Interview with Yasintha Banda, Mnthemba Village, Katete, Zambia, 8th August, 2008

gold and ivory at a public ceremony that came to be known as Kulamba, or "thanksgiving". In publicly expressing their gratitude to Kalonga, the sub-chiefs demonstrated their political allegiance to their benefactor, hence reinforcing his prestige, authority and power. Moreover, the ceremony welded the junior traditional rulers to Kalonga and his successors.

If Kulamba commenced as a means of binding the Maravi ruling class together, it over time came to perform other equally vital functions. According to oral testimonies, the ceremony became the foundation of redistributive politics in the Maravi-Chewa kingdom, and later in Kalonga Gawa Undi's empire. Through the ceremony, Kalonga and his successors, who also inherited his title, redistributed tribute to various parts of the kingdom to meet the needs of their subjects. For example, the overlord sent part of the food he received during the ceremony from food-rich to food-short areas that may have been struck by drought or famine. Kulamba thus served as a principle vehicle of relief distribution. This fostered economic interdependence between various areas under Kalonga's control, with his court serving as a clearing house.[14]

It may be evident from the foregoing that the Kulamba ceremony occupied a central place in the cultural, economic and political life of the Chewa long before the imposition of colonial hegemony. But its significance was lost on British and Portuguese colonial authorities and missionaries in central Africa during the 19th century. Unable to discern it social, economic and political functions, missionaries in particular routinely condemned Kulamba with its Gule Wamkulu (Nyau) dance and rituals as a licentious and "pagan" activity that encouraged immorality and hence undermined African faith in Christianity. Their antipathy toward the ceremony was reinforced by the fact that in both colonial Zambia and Malawi performers of the Gule Wamkulu or Nyau dance, the hallmark of the Kulamba event, stubbornly resisted conversion to Christianity. It was in this light that European missionaries in the former territory successfully lobbied the colonial government to proscribe it in 1934.[15]

Kulamba Ceremony since 1984: the Role of Kalonga Gawa Undi X

Apart from missionary opposition to Kulamba ceremony, there were several reasons which accounted for the proscription of Kulamba ceremony by the colonial administration. An informant recently recalled that the practice of paying homage and tribute to the Chewa Paramount portended

[14] Lameck Daka and G. Chigwala interviews cited.
[15] Mwanawasa, "Speech".

disloyalty to the colonial state and was tantamount to idol worship. This, the informant added, was too much for the colonisers to bear. Afraid that the paying of tribute to chiefs would undermine the colonial state, imperial authorities banned Kulamba in 1934. In spite of the ban, however, Chewa subordinate chiefs apparently continued to forward tribute to their superior, albeit clandestinely.

After its ban by colonial authorities in 1934, Kulamba fell into abeyance for the next five decades. In early 1984, however, Kalonga Kalonga Gawa Undi X invited Chewa chiefs from Mozambique, Zambia and Malawi to Mkaika palace in Katete, Zambia so that they would revive the Kulamba ceremony. The Paramount Chief further lobbied the governments in Zambia and in her two neighbouring countries to win their support for the restoration of the ceremony.[16] When his sub-chiefs chiefs met at Mkaika palace in the same year, they unanimously agreed that the Kulamba ceremony should be held annually in Zambia at the palace during the last Saturday of August.[17] 1984 therefore marked the revival of Kulamba. Since then, it has occupied a high place in the cultural calendar of the Chewa people of all the three countries, a point that was most poignantly made by the late President Levy Patrick Mwanawasa when he attended the Kulamba ceremony in 2007.[18]

In view of his commitment to Christianity, it is not unsurprising that Kalonga Gawa Undi X played such a pivotal role in the revival of the Kulamba traditional ceremony.[19] It is tempting to see his role in the restoration of the cultural form as an indication of the waning influence of European missionaries over the aging Paramount Chief. But there is no empirical evidence to prove this assertion. For Kalonga Gawa Undi X himself remained a devout Christian well up to his death in 2004. The answer to the puzzle as to why he resuscitated the "pagan" ceremony seems to lie in the fact Gawa Undi X perceived no incongruity between indigenous cultural forms and Christian beliefs and praxis. As may be recalled from chapter 2 in this volume, the Chewa suzerain comprehended Christianity through pre-existing Chewa cultural and belief systems. Thus, he did not share European missionaries' revulsion towards African culture. Nor did he dismiss its related rituals and dances as the root of African paganism, as

---

16 Joseph Galeta Chikuta, Senior Induna to Kalonga Gawa Undi, Mkaika Palace, Katete, Zambia, 6 August, 2008.

17 Joseph Galeta Chikuta, interview cited.

18 Mwanawasa, "Speech".

19 The early life, career and religious beliefs of Kalonga Gawa Undi X have been discussed in considerable details in another chapter in this book.

missionaries often complained.

Oral accounts strongly suggest that the overlord's central objective in reviving the Kulamba was to preserve Chewa cultural identity against such forces as urbanisation and what he saw as morally corrosive foreign influences that by the 1980s were deeply encroaching upon local cultural identity.[20] According to oral testimonies, Kalonga Gawa Undi X had by then realised that young boys and girls in Zambia and beyond were falling prey to alien influences, losing their respect for their culture, and hence growing up without appreciating what was culturally expected of them as Africans.[21] By 1984, he seems to have become convinced that reviving the ceremony would provide his subjects in Zambia, Malawi and Mozambique with an effective medium through which they could preserve their cultural values, customs, beliefs and heritage for posterity.[22]

It is significant to stress that although the faith of the Chewa ruler in Christianity was unquestionable, he did not jettison his traditional culture. He realised that the Kulamba ceremony was central to protecting local cultural values, notwithstanding his belief in Christianity and modernity. To the old freedom fighter, the revival of the ceremony was, therefore, not merely an act of cultural preservation but also cultural patriotism. Yet it would be a mistake to think that cultural considerations were the only driving force behind the Paramount Chief's call for the restoration of the ceremony. It seems plausible, too, that economic and geopolitical considerations similarly weighed heavily on his mind when he called upon other Chewa chiefs in the three territories and their governments to resuscitate Kulamba.

By the 1980s, as may be recalled from an earlier chapter, Kalonga Gawa Undi X had become deeply concerned with Zambia's worsening economic malaise. He had by then indeed concluded that the post-colonial state in Zambia alone was incapable of redressing the growing impoverishment of the country. There are indications that from the 1980s onward, the Paramount Chief felt that strengthening economic and political ties between countries in southern Africa was one of the possible remedies to Zambia's economic woes.[23] If this view is correct, it explains why he eagerly solicited the backing of the governments of Zambia, Malawi and Mozambique when he first mooted the idea of reviving the Kulamba ceremony in 1984. The

---

[20] Teddy Sakala, Lameck Daka, Edward Nyirongo and Kaseke Phiri , interviews cited.
[21] Yasintha Banda and Headman Chigwala, interviews cited.
[22] Joseph Galeta Chikuta, interview cited.
[23] Ibid.

Chewa Paramount Chief must have believed that the restoration of the ceremony would strengthen the cultural and economic bonds between Zambia and her neighbours. This would in turn reinforce their trade relations. Stated in other words, in reviving the Kulamba ceremony, Kalonga Gawa Undi X sought to construct a cultural space within which economic relations between Zambia and other southern Africa countries would blossom or flourish.

The Kulamba Ceremony Today

It is in the context of the Paramount Chief's economic and geo-political concerns that one may appreciate the transformations that have occurred in the Kulamba ceremony since its revival in 1984. It may be recalled that during the pre-colonial and for most of the colonial days before it was outlawed in 1984, the traditional ceremony was performed by individual chiefs and their subjects on different occasions.[24] In 1984, however, Kalonga Gawa Undi X and other Chewa chiefs from Mozambique, Malawi and Zambia all agreed to transform the Kulamba traditional event into an annual event. Henceforth, it would be (and has been) attended by all Chewa chiefs and their subjects at the same time at Mkaika palace, the traditional headquarters of Kalonga Gawa Undi, eight kilometres outside Katete district and about 480 km east of Lusaka.[25] Needless to say, this was calculated to foster greater cultural cohesion, promote trade, and thus strengthen economic integration between the three nations.[26] Since its resuscitation in 1984, then, the ceremony has taken on an international character. It has thus been transformed into an integrative force that annually brings together thousands of Chewa and non-Chewa people from Zambia, Malawi and Mozambique to Mkaika.

How is the ceremony performed today? Three days before the event takes place, in the last week of August, Chewa chiefs from Malawi, Mozambique and Zambia converge at Mkaika to prepare for the actual day of the ceremony. On the eve of the ceremony, the Paramount Chief himself is taken to an isolated place known as Gwalada, where he spends the night alone. Gwalada is strictly out-of-bounds, especially to all women, including the Paramount Chief's wife. In the morning, the Paramount Chief leaves his

[24] Interview with Edward Nyirongo, Grandson of Gawa Undi X, Mkaika palace, Katete, 6 August, 2008. Galeta Galeta Chikuta, interview cited.
[25] See Nebert Mulenga, "Discerning the Different Faces of Kulamba, Kulamba Kubwalo," http://www.times.co.zm/news/viewnews.cgi? category.
[26] Joseph Gareta Chikutaand Edward Nyirongo interviews cited. See also Andrew Lungu, 'Harmony Provided Through Kulamba Traditional Ceremony', (link needed) The current practice of Kulamba took shape after the ceremony was revived in 1984.

royal retreat to join his subjects at the main arena near the palace. He is escorted there by his indunas (councillors) and by a retinue of dancers and musicians.[27]

Protocol demands that before all the invited guests are seated, Nyangu, the Queen Mother, first takes her place in her special shelter within the arena known as the Dzimbabwe. She is escorted there by female singers and dancers. Also in the company of the Nyangu are the Anamwali or girl initiates covered in chitenge cloth to conceal their partial nudity. When the Nyangu has taken her seat on the reed mat in the shelter, the Paramount Chief takes his place on a raised platform.[28]

A group of colourful Nyau dancers wearing masks marches in style to take up their positions close to the platform. Accompanied by a kaligo player with his enchanting music played on the Chewa traditional harp, subordinated chiefs proceed to take a glance at the overlord. The Paramount Chief then goes into Dzimbabwe to greet the Nyangu and her attendants, after which he takes to his seat between two lion emblems. Sitting in state, the Chewa potentate listens attentively as his speech is delivered to his citizens and invited guests through his induna. Through the speech, the suzerain greets his people and welcomes them to the Kulamba ceremony. Afterwards, he and the gathering listen to speeches from government officials.[29] To break the monotony of speeches, the people are treated to dancing by the Chinamwali girls with bare breasts and beaded skirts. These are girls who have recently matured into womanhood. The Kulamba ceremony thus serves as an occasion when they are shown to the public through dance and song. The members of the public throng the dance arena to shower the girls with tokens of appreciation, in modern days usually money. The Chinamwali dance that marks the official opening of the floor. It is after this dance the subordinate chiefs perform the Kulamba ritual, which consists in paying tribute to their sovereign.

The chiefs' tribute today comprises a wide range of items. These include foodstuffs such as mealie-meal, fish, maize grain, groundnuts and livestock like cows, goats and sheep. Other gifts are money, bark cloth, animal skins and mats, but some forms of tribute are concealed from public

---

[27] Enestle Zimba, 'Discover Kulamba, a Three Nation Traditional Ceremony' http:www.zambia-the African-safari.com/africas.

[28] Edward Nyirongo, interview cited.

[29] Usually, the governments of Malawi, Mozambique and Zambia are represented at the ceremony. However, the last Kulamba held in 2007 was unique as presidents of the three countries, Mbingu Wamutharika, Armando Emilio Guebuza and Levy Mwanawasa, respectively, graced the ceremony.

view.[30] In return, the Chewa potentate thanks his subjects and sometimes offers his walking stick (ndodo or nkholi) to whoever he wishes. This concept of paying tribute, which is also practised by other cultural groups such as the Bemba, Lunda, Lenje and Lozi is a clear expression of respect to Kalonga Gawa Undi. Additionally, the presentation of gifts is a powerful statement that draws the attention of the Paramount Chief to the economic fortunes or misfortunes of various chiefdoms under the potentate.

Apart from paying homage and giving gifts to the Kalonga, subordinate chiefs also present reports on socio-economic activities that have taken place their areas since the previous ceremony. The reports shed light on the general welfare of the people in the traditional rulers' respective chiefdoms. In the reports, sub-chiefs explain the successes they have scored as well as the challenges faced by their subjects. These challenges presented to Kalonga Gawa Undi include among others, the inadequate provision of educational facilities such as schools and teachers, the absence of clean drinking water and poor communication facilities like roads.[31]

The Kulamba ceremony has thus taken on new characteristics and functions in order to meet the challenges and demands of the modern world. It has become a forum at which the Chewa people bring the difficulties that beset them to a wider audience and world. Indeed, their Paramount Chief uses the occasion to appeal for government's intervention to resolve the difficulties that beset his subjects.[32]

Gule Wamkulu (Nyau)

The hallmark of the Kulamba ceremony is the famous Gule Wamkulu dance. Performed by masked Nyau dancers, Gule Wamkulu constitutes the main dance of the ceremony. The term 'Gule Wamkulu' means "the great dance". Prior to the dance itself, its performers observe a series of secret rituals associated with the Nyau society, whose member form a secret brotherhood believed to foster the link between the living and the living dead. The term Nyau is also sometimes used to refer to the dance itself and to the various types of attire won by the dancers during the performance.[33]

It is perhaps more appropriate to think of the Gule Wamkulu, whose

---

[30] Interview with Teddy Abraham Sakala, Presiding Court Justice, Kawaza Old Local Court Grade A, Kagoro Sub Centre, Katete, Zambia, 8th August, 2008; Interview with Levison Phiri, Headman Mutantauzi and Handsen Daka, Headman Mutentemuka, at Katawa Basic School, Katete, Zambia, 9th August, 2008 and Lameck Daka interview cited.

[31] Joseph Galeta Chikuta interview cited.

[32] Edward Nyirongo interview cited

[33] Mtonga, "the Drama of Gule Wamkulu", p. 110; see also Schoffelleers and Linden, "The Resistance of Nyau Societies," p. 257.

dancers are referred to as Vilombo ("animals"), as an amalgam of dances. This is because along the Gule Wamkulu dances there are other different types of dances that are simultaneously performed. Prominent among them are Chimtali, Chinamwali, Chihoda, Chimbumbuli, Chiwele, Chikanke, Chimbano and Makanja.[34] A large number of these dances are performed during the Kulamba ceremony, but some of them take place only during such specific occasions as funerals or weddings.

Dances performed under the rubric of Gule Wamkulu are performed to the accompaniment of different types of drumming. Each dance is characterised by its own specific drum beat. For instance, there is a particular form of drumming for dances involving synchronized body movements. In other performances, dancers may display their dancing prowess as they climbs a tall pole.[35] Groups of Gule Wamkulu artists are presented to Kalonga Gawa Undi by their respective chiefs. They all engage in a stiff competition in an attempt to show the Paramount Chief that they have the best dancers.[36] As they perform before their overlord, they not only pay homage to the king but they also reinforce his social standing and authority.

It is significant to note that although the Gule Wamkulu (Nyau) is shrouded in mystery, it is the most revered dance which appeals to young Chewa men aspiring to join the secret society. There are several reasons which compel men to join the society. Within the Chewa cultural context, the Nyau brotherhood society is a privileged group through which its members enhance their own social status and prestige.[37] Moreover, enlisting in the brotherhood serves as a rite of passage into socially recognised adulthood and publicly marks one's masculinity.[38]

National and Regional Integration

It may be apparent from the foregoing remarks that organisationally and functionally, the Kulamba cultural ceremony has since its restoration been transformed. While it retains some of its age-old functions such as reinforcing their sovereign's prestige and power, the cultural ceremony now also serves as a medium through which the Chewa-speaking people

[34] Chikuta interview cited, interview with Yohanne Banda at Mnthemba Village, Katete, Zambia, 8th August, 2008. (This informant joined the Nyau secret society). Also interview with Mailes Moyo at Chingaipe Village, Katete, 8th August, 2008., interview with Kaseske Phiri, Farmer, at Chingaipe village, Katete, Zambia, 8th august, 2008; Interview with Yasintha Banda, at Mnthemba Village,Katete Zambia, 8th August, 2008.,Sakala interview cited.

[35] Lameck Daka, interview cited.

[36] Chikuta interview cited

[37] Yohanne Banda interview cited, and Chimbelekelo interview cited.

[38] Banda interview cited.

interact with the wider world. From this standpoint, it is easy to appreciate why the ceremony today occupies a high position in the economic and political imagination of not just among the Chewa people but also leading political authorities and economic planners in Zambia and other parts of southern Africa. To these people, the Kulamba ceremony is an instrument for championing economic development and integration in southern Africa. The late President Levy Patrick Mwanawasa made this point most power-fully in his speech at Mkaika, Katete, in 2007. The ceremony, the President noted, was a powerful tool with which Zambia and her neighbours could attract tourists and investors, leading to "infrastructural development" and the creation of employment in the region.[39]

As Kalonga Gawa Undi X had intended, the cultural event has further become a medium of economic integration in southern Africa. Indeed, it is an occasion during which trading activity between ordinary people from Mozambique, Zambia and Malawi reaches its feverish peak in Katete, with national and multi-national corporations operating the region as a whole actively advertising their businesses.[40] This because the ceremony attracts thousands of Chewa and non-Chewa-speaking people. The latter include chiefs from various chieftainships in Zambia and even regional leaders as was the case in 2007 when President Mwanawasa of Zambia, Mbingu Wa Mutharika of Malawi and Armando Emilio Guebuza of Mozambique at-tended the ceremony at Mkaika.[41] Prominent among the attendees are also opposition leaders.[42]

The Kulamba ceremony draws people from a wide spectrum of society in Zambia and in neighbouring territories. From this standpoint, it serves a focal point of regional economic and political integration. This point is not lost on politicians in the region. In 2007, President Mwanawasa recognised the integrative potential of the cultural ceremony, which, he noted, enables the Chewa and other people to "live in unity as one people." For this reason, he committed his government to promoting the ceremony and other relat-ed cultural events.[43]

Mwanawasa's dedication to enhancing traditional ceremonies reflect-ed his realisation that such events were a means of cultivating warm, harmonious and friendly relationship between neighbouring countries.

---

[39] Mwanawasa, "Speech".
[40] Joseph Galeta Chikuta Mbewe, interview cited
[41] Mwanawasa, "Speech".
[42] See *The Post*, 15 September 2008.
[43] Mwanawas, "Speech".

Indeed, since its revival in 1984, the Kulamba traditional ceremony has contributed in strengthening social, political and economic ties between people in the region. The usefulness of the ceremony as an instrument of regional integration lies in the fact that it provides a common ground for the ten million Chewa people who today inhabit Malawi, Mozambique and Zambia and who all look to Kalonga Gawa Undi as their sovereign.[44] This makes obsolete the artificial boundaries that imperial powers carved between the three territories in the 19th century.

Today, Kulamba also acts as a vehicle of nation-building and political cohesion. This observation is vindicated by the fact the annual cultural event is attended by non-Chewa speaking ethnic groups from all over Zambia. For instance, in 2007 and 2008 the Litunga (king) of the Lozi people, Paramount Chief Chitimukulu of the Bemba, Senior Chief Ishinde of the Lunda, Senior Chief Mukuni of the Toka Leya, and Tonga chiefs from Southern province either participated in or sent their representatives to attend the Kulamba in Katete. Within Eastern province, the Nsenga, Tumbuka and the Ngoni also annually attend the Kulamba ceremony. At the ceremony, the Nsenga and the Tumbuka field their own dance troupes, respectively known as Chinsongwe and Fwemba.[45] The participation of non-Chewa speakers not only affords them an opportunity to observe at close quarters how the Chewa conduct their traditional ceremony. It also enhances understanding, cooperation and goodwill between the Chewa and other people. The fact that chiefs from all corners of Zambia attend the Kulamba ceremony strengthens national unity and contributes to minimising inter-ethnic rivalry.[46]

Economically speaking, Kulamba and other traditional ceremonies are a platform for bolstering inter- and intra-regional economic integration. This point is not lost on politicians, economic planners and such regional economic blocks as the Southern African Development Community (SADC). As President Levy Patrick Mwanawasa's 2007 speech at Mkaika strongly suggests, regional leaders and economic blocks do appreciate that African culture and traditional leadership at the grassroots roots level are the foundation of genuine economic development.[47] To regional leaders and organisations, internal and external economic ties are bound to be

---

[44] Mwanawas, "Speech".

[45] Headman Chigwala, Lameck Daka, Teddy Sakala, Mailes Moyo, Chikuta, Handsen Daka and Levison Phiri, interviews cited.

[46] Joseph Galeta Chikuta interview cited.

[47] Joseph Galeta Chikuta Mbewe interview cited.

strengthened and fruitful when they are anchored to African culture and practices.

It is no surprise, then, that the Kulamba ceremony is now perceived by economic planners and politicians alike as one of the cornerstones of the Zambia-Malawi-Mozambique Growth Triangle (ZMM-GT) initiative. Explaining the background to the initiative, Listard Banda argues that

> The background and concept of Growth Triangle is to promote economic cooperation and to accelerate the pace of development among the countries of Zambia, Malawi and Mozambique. This is an initiative of the United Nations Development Program ZMM-GT Project of 1999 under its Africa programme for innovative cooperation among the south (PICAS). The area covered by the project includes north and eastern Zambia, central and northern Malawi and western Mozambique particularly Tete province. To this end, the project covers the entire Chewa kingdom in Zambia, Malawi and Mozambique. The concept of ZMM-GT Project places the private sector at the centre of growth mechanism.[48]

Since the ZMM-GT project covers the entire region of the Chewa kingdom, it has also won the blessings of the Chewa Royal Establishment. Like economic planners, Chewa traditional leaders perceive the project is an avenue for expanding trade, promoting economic cooperation and hence accelerating the pace of development in areas under their jurisdiction.[49] It is in the same vein that the Royal Establishment and the political rulers in Zambia, Malawi and Mozambique have welcomed the Chipata-Mchinji rail, which is aimed at boosting the movement of goods and people throughout the region.[50]

Conclusion

The call by Kalonga Gawa Undi X to revive the Kulamba ceremony of the Chewa in 1984 was motivated by cultural, economic and geo-political concerns. Certainly the erosion of African culture by rising urbanisation, industrialisation and other outside influences was of great concern to the Paramount Chief. Thus, even though the traditional ceremony was dismissed by missionaries as the citadel of African cultural degradation and sloth and had also been banned for over fifty years, the Christian Chief actively campaigned for its restoration in the 1980s. His campaign for the resuscitation of the ceremony was an act of cultural patriotism. Through

---

[48] Banda, Chewa Kingom, p. 35.
[49] Lizzy Ngobeka, 'Chewas in Grand Celebration of Historical Kulamba Meet' http://www.times.co.zm/.
[50] Mwanawasa, "Speech".

Kulamba, he hoped that his followers in Malawi, Mozambique and Zambia could preserve their cultural heritage and thus insulate themselves from morally corrosive influences.

But even if conceived of as a Chewa cultural space, the Kulamba traditional ceremony is now more than just an ethnic affair. Since its revival in 1984, it has taken on new meanings, new attributes and new functions. To economic planners, to politicians and to chiefs alike, it offers a platform essential to uplifting the economic, social and political welfare of people in southern Africa as a whole. In Zambia alone, it contributes to emasculating ethnic differentiation and rivalry through annually bringing together the Chewa and non-Chewa people from all corners of Zambia and even beyond. Thus, though commonly comprehended as a Chewa cultural affair, the Kulamba ceremony today is a viable instrument for promoting national and regional integration.

7

Conclusion

The architects of the historiography of African traditional authorities in colonial and post-colonial settings have all too often stereotyped chiefs as little more than instruments of political control and subjugation.[1] The architects of this discourse certainly recognise the important role of chiefs during the colonial era and in contemporary Africa. They, however, maintain that during the imperial period, the chiefly office was neither democratised nor strengthened to champion the welfare of the subjects of empire. To the contrary, the exponents of this discourse hold that chiefs became agents of centralised power and therefore participated in their own subjugation at the hands of colonial powers and authorities. To these academics, the attainment of independence in Africa in the 1950s and 1960s brought no noticeable change in how traditional authorities related to state power. This argument has most forcefully been made by Mahood Mamdani, who emphatically insists that although independence de-racialised the political space, it did not necessarily democratise traditional political institutions and customary law. To the Ugandan scholar, these undemocratic institutions and customary law have in fact been usurped by post-colonial rulers in Africa to buttress their dictatorial hold on power, often in league with chiefs.[2]

Obliviously, it cannot be denied that some indigenous rulers in colonial and post-colonial Africa have historically served the interests of centralised power. Such rulers may thus be unreservedly dismissed as having been allies of those who have wielded social, political and economic power both before and after independence in Africa. Such chiefs, from this standpoint, can be said to have been accomplices in their own and the domina-

---
[1] See chapter 2.
[2] See Mahmood Mamdani, *Citizen and Subject: Contemporary Africa and the Legacy of Late Colonialism* (Princeton: Princeton University Press, 1996).

tion of their subjects. Yet in casting traditional authorities in this light, this discourse obscures the fundamental differences in the opinions, ideologies and practices chiefs have displayed towards centralised control since the imposition of Western hegemony in Africa. Moreover, academic discourse that treats traditional authorities as passive agents of state power masks the complex ways indigenous rulers in Africa have drawn on centralised political institutions to defend their chiefly office, and hence their own interests, authority and power.

Focused on the life of Kalonga Gawa Undi X, whose reign spanned the colonial and post-colonial period between 1943 and 1964, this study may be read as a corrective to academic studies that portray African chiefs as no more than pawns of state control. Born at the peak of British political hegemony in Africa in the 1930s, the Chewa Paramount Chief's life and political career were as much informed by colonial rule itself as his ideologies and praxis were shaped by his cultural heritage. To be sure, Kalonga Gawa Undi X initially embraced colonial institutions, including Native Authorities, education and Christianity. But this was because the Chewa Paramount Chief perceived these institutions as viable vehicles by which the colonised could improve their socio-economic well-being and, simultaneously, challenge state power.

Nowhere was Western colonialism designed to benefit its victims, a point that seems to have dawned on Kalonga Gawa Undi X in the late 1950s. It is this realization that undoubtedly propelled him to enlist in the nationalist struggle for freedom from Britain once he returned home from his overseas training in 1957. In a paradoxical twist, the Chewa sovereign, unlike the urban-based nationalist elite, waged the anti-colonial protest through the institutions forged by the coloniser. This was certainly because he believed that these institutions could be deployed to both ameliorate the welfare of his people and, as noted above, to undermine colonial domination. It is in this light that we may appreciate why the Chewa sovereign carried out the reforms discussed earlier in this volume. Through these reforms, the Paramount Chief-cum-nationalist filled Native Authorities under his control with pro-nationalist sympathizers in the late 1950s, who enormously contributed to bringing down the Union Jack in 1964.

Strong evidence indicates that the suzerain's ambiguous disposition towards imperial power with its allied institutions spilled over into the post-colonial era from 1964 onward. Just as he had earlier employed colonial institutions to undermine European rule and to uplift the socio-economic well-being of his people, so did Kalonga Gawa Undi X deploy their post-colonial counterparts to concretise the social, economic and political gains of independence. This, of course, meant that the potentate worked within the realm of institutions that the new Zambian ruling elites crafted. But if the architects of post-colonial institutions perceived them as means to monopolise power, the Paramount Chief saw them as an instrument for advancing the welfare of his people and to protect the political autonomy of the chiefly office after independence.

Kalonga Gawa Undi, therefore, pushed and pulled at the boundaries of colonial and post-colonial power to shape his destiny and that of his subjects. It would thus be grossly misleading to dismiss him as a passive collaborator of centralised power. Evidence provided in this study aptly demonstrates that the potentate was not slow to condemn the excesses of successive regimes in colonial and post-colonial Zambia whenever they passed legislation that threatened to eclipse the political influence of traditional rulers and undermine their prestige or prerogatives. In the same vein, in 1984 he revived the Kulamba ceremony even though he was a committed convert to Christianity and white missionaries had condemned the ceremony as the fortress of African "paganism". His life, career and practices therefore call for an urgent reinterpretation of the academic scholarship that indiscriminately caricatures chiefs in Africa as no more than pawns in the hands of state power, colonial or post-colonial.

BIBLIOGRAPHY

Primary Sources

National Archives of Zambia (arranged chronologically)

(i) Eastern Province Series
EP 4/7/13, Paramount Chief Undi, 1952-1954
EP 1//1/12, Chiefs and Headmen, General, 1952-1965.
EP 1/1/1/36, Fort Jameson Newsletter, Kuunika, 1956-1962.
EP 1/1/19, Land Leases, White Fathers, 1959-1966.
EP 1/1/1/54, House of Chiefs, 1962- 1973.
EP 1/1/55, Tour Reports, 1962-1972.
EP 1/1/62, Chipata Rural Council, 1964-1969.
EP 1/1/63, Natural Resources, 1964-1973.
EP 4/10/18, Development Seminars, 1967-1972.
EP 4/1/98, Development Committees, 1969.

(ii) Secretariat Series
Sec2/705, Katete Tour Reports, 1951.
Sec2/706, Katete Tour Reports, 1952.
Sec2/694, Fort Jameson Tour Reports 1952.
Sec2/ 708, Katete Tour Reports, 1954-1956.
Sec2/709, Katete Tour Report, 1956.
Sec2/707, Katete Tour Reports, 1957.
Sec2/708, Katete Tour Reports, 1957.
Sec2/710, Katete Tour Reports, 1957.
Sec2/711, Katete Tour Reports, 1958.
Sec2/712, Katete Tour Report, 1959.

(iii) Government Documents
Northern Rhodesia, *African Affairs Annual Report for the Year 1951*. Lusaka: Government Printer, 1952.
Northern Rhodesia, *African Affairs Annual Report for the Year 1953*. Lusaka: Government Printer, 1954.
Northern Rhodesia, *African Affairs Annual Report for the Year 1954*. Lusaka: Government Printer 1955.
Northern Rhodesia, *African Affairs Annual Report for the Year 1956*. Lusaka:

Bibliography

Government Printer, 1957.

Northern Rhodesia, *African Affairs Annual Report for the Year 1957*. Lusaka: Government Printer, 1959.

Northern Rhodesia, *African Affairs Annual Report for the Year 1958*. Lusaka: Government Printer, 1959.

Northern Rhodesia, *African Affairs Annual Report for the Year 1959*. Lusaka: Government Printer, 1960.

Northern Rhodesia, *African Affairs Annual Report for the Year 1960*. Lusaka: Government Printer, 1961.

(iv) Newspapers

The Post

Times of Zambia

Secondary Sources

(i) Books and Articles

Akyeampong, Emmanuel. "Christianity, Modernity and the Weight of Tradition in the Life of Asantehene Agyeman Prempeh I, c. 1888-1931." *Africa* 69, 2 (1999), pp. 279-311.

Aluko, Olajide. "Politics of Decolonisation in British West Africa, 1945-1960," in J.F. Ade Ajayi and Michael Crowder (eds.), *History of West Africa* Vol. Two. Essex: Longman Group Ltd., 1968.

Banda, Listard Elifala. *The Chewa Kingdom*. Lusaka: Desert Enterprises Limited. 2002.

Bates, Robert H. *Rural Responses to Industrialization: A Study of Village Zambia*. New Haven: Yale University Press, 1976.

Berry, Sara S. "Unsettled Accounts: Stool Debts, Chieftaincy Disputes and the Question of Asante Constitutionalism." *Journal of African History* 39 (1998), pp. 39-62.

_____. *Chiefs Know their Boundaries: Essays on the Property, Power, and the Past in Asante, 1896-1996*. Portsmouth NH: Heinemann; Oxford: James Currey and Cape Town: David Philip, 2001.

Boahen, Adu. *African Perspectives on Colonialism*. Baltimore: Johns Hopkins University Press, 1978.

Bradley, Kenneth. *Once a District Officer*. New York: St Martin's Press, 1966.

Calvocoressi, Peter. *World Politics since 1945*. Sixth Edition. London and New York. 1968.

Chanock, Martin. Law, *Custom and Social Order: The Colonial Experience in Malawi and Zambia* (Cambridge: Cambridge University Press, 1985

Chinyanta, M. and C.J. Mwale. *Mutomboko Ceremony and Kazembe Dynasty*. Lusaka: Kenneth Kaunda Foundation, 1989.

Chipungu, Samuel N. *The State, Technology and Peasant Differentiation in Zambia: A Study of Southern Province*. Lusaka: Historical Association of Zambia. 1992.

_____. "African Leadership under Indirect Rule in Colonial Zambia," in

Samuel N. Chipungu (ed.), *Guardians in their Time: Experiences of Zambians under Colonial Rule, 1890-1964.* London: Macmillan, 1992, pp. 50-73.

_____."Accumulation from within: The Boma Class and Native Treasury in colonial Zambia," in Chipungu (ed.), *Guardians in their Time,* pp. 74-96.

Comaroff, Jean and John Comaroff, *Of Revelation and Revolution: Christianity, Colonialism and Consciousness in South Africa* Vol. One. Chicago and London: The Chicago University Press, 1991.

Cooper, Frederick. *Decolonization and African Society: The Labor Question in French and British Africa.* Cambridge: Cambridge University Press, 1996.

Deroche, Andrew J. "You can't fight guns with knives," in Gewald, Jan-Bart, Marja Hinfelaar and Giacomo Macola (eds.) "Introduction," in Jan-Bart, Marja Honfelaar and Giacomo Macola (eds.). *One Zambia, Many Histories: Towards a History of Post-colonial Zambia.* Leiden and London: Brill, 2008, pp. 76-97.

Dixon-Fyle, Mac. "The Seventh Day Adventists (S.A.D) in the Protest Politics of the Tonga Plateau, Northern Rhodesia." *African Social Research* 26, 1 (1978,pp. 453-467.

Elbourne, Elizabeth. "Early Khoisan Uses of Mission Christianity," in Henry Bredekamp and Robert Ross (eds.), *Missions and Christianity in South African History.* Johannesburg: Witwatersrand University Press, 1995.

Fay, Gadsden. "Education and Society in Colonial Zambia," in Chipungu (ed.), *Guardians in their Time,* pp. 97-125.

Ferguson, James. *Expectations of Modernity: Myths and Meanings of Urban Life on the Zambian Copperbelt.* Berkeley, Los Angeles, and London: University of California Press, 1999.

Gewald, Hinfelaar and Macola."Introduction," in Gewald, Hinfelaar and Macola(eds.), *One Zambia,* pp. 1-16.

Gertzel, Cherry and Morris Szeftel." Politics in an African urban setting: the role of the Copperbelt in the Transition to the One Party state, 1964-1973, " in Cherry Gertzel, Carolyn Baylies and Morris Szeftel (eds.) *The Dynamics of the One-party state in Zambia.* Manchester: Manchester University Press, 1984

Gibson, Richard. *African Liberation Movements: Contemporary Struggles against White Minority Rule.* London, Oxford and New York: Oxford University Press, 1972.

Good, Robert C. *U.D.I.: The International Politics of the Rhodesian Rebellion.* London: Faber and Faber, 1973.

Gould, Jeremy. "Subsidiary sovereignty and the constitution of political space in Zambia," in Gewald, Hinfelaar and Macola (eds.) *One Zambia.*

Hall, Richard. *The High Price of Principles: Kaunda and the White South.* London: Hodder and Stoughton, 1969.

Harries, Patrick. "Missionaries, Marxists, and Magic: Power and the Politics of Literacy in South-East Africa," *Journal of Southern African Studies* 23, 3 (2001), pp. 405-427.

Bibliography

_____. *Work, Culture, and Identity: Migrant Laborers in Mozambique and South Africa, c. 1860-1910.* Portsmouth NH: Heinemann; Johannesburg: Witwatersrand University Press, and London: James Currey, 1994.

_____. *Butterflies and Barbarians: Swiss Missionaries and Systems of Knowledge in South-East Africa.* Harare: Weaver; Johannesburg: Witswatersrand University Press and Athens: Ohio University Press, 2007.

Harris-Jones, Peter, *Freedom and Labour Mobilization and Political Control on the Zambian Copperbelt.* Oxford: Basil Blackwell, 1975.

Hobsbawm, Eric and Terence Ranger (eds.), *The Invention of Tradition.* Cambridge: Cambridge University Press, 1983.

Illife, John. "The Age of Improvement and Differentiation," in I.N. Kimambo and A. Temu (eds.), *A History of Tanzania* (Nairobi: East African Publishing House, 1969, pp. 123-160.

Isaacman, Allen. "Peasants and the Rural Social Protest in Africa." Paper commissioned for the Joint ACLS-SSRC Committee presented at the African Studies Annual General Conference, 2-6 November 1989, Atlanta, Georgia, USA.

Isaacman, Allen and Derek Peterson. "Making the Chikunda: Military Slavery and Ethnicity in Southern Africa, 1750-1900." *International Journal of African Historical Studies* 36, 2 (2003), pp. 257-281.

Kalusa, Walima T. "Language, Medical Missionaries, and the Re-Interpretation of Missionary Medicine in Colonial Mwinilunga, 1922-1951." *Journal of Eastern African Studies* 1, 1 (2007), pp. 57-78.

_____. "From an Agency of Cultural Destruction to an Agency of Public Health: Transformations in Catholic Missionary Medicine in Post-Colonial Zambia, 1964-1982. Paper presented at the Joint Conference held in Freiburg, Germany, and Basel, Switzerland, 14-17 May 2008.

_____. "Eastern Zambia in the Liberation of Mozambique, 1962-1989," Lusaka: Manuscript, Hashim Mbita Project, 2008.

Kamana, Dustan W. "Zambia," in Douglas G. Anglin, Timothy M. Shawa and Carl G Widstrand (eds.), *Conflict and Change in Southern Africa: Papers from a Scandinavian-Canadian Conference.* Washington DC.: University Press of America, 1978, pp. 33-68.

Kemp, Amanda D and Robert Trent Vinson, "'Poking Holes in the Sky': Professor James Thaele, American Negroes, and Modernity in Segregationist South Africa." *African Studies Review* 43, 1 (2000), pp.141-159.

Larmer, Miles. "'A little bit like a volcano': The United Progressive Party and Resistance to One-Party Rule in Zambia, 1964-1980," *International Journal of African Historical Studies* 39 (2006).

_____. "Enemies within?: Opposition to the Zambian one-party State, 1972-1980," in Gewald, Hinfelaar and Macola" (eds.) *One Zambia, Many Histories.* pp. 98-128.

Landau, Paul Stuart. *Realm of the Word: Language, Gender, Christianity in a Southern African Kingdom.* Portsmouth NH: Heinemann; Cape Town: David Philip, and London: James Currey, 1995.

Larson, Pier M. "'Capacities and Modes of Thinking': Intellectual Engagements and Subaltern Hegemony in Early Malagasy Christianity," *American Historical Review* 104, 4 (1997), pp. 969-1002.

Linden, Ian. "Chewa Initiation Rites and Nyau Societies: The Use of Religious Institutions in Local Politics at Mau," in T.O. Ranger and John Weller (eds.), *Themes in the Christian History of Central Africa*. Lusaka: Heinemann, 1975, pp. 330-45.

Linden, Ian and Jane Linden. *Catholics, Peasants and Chewa Resistance in Nyasaland, 1889-1939*. London: Heinemann, 1974.

Macola, Giacomo. *The Kingdom of Kazembe: History and Politics in North-Eastern Zambia and Katanga to 1950*. Munster, Hamburg and London: Lit Verlag, 2002.

_____. "Harry Mwaanga Nkumbula, UNIP and the roots Of authoritarianism in nationalist Zambia," in Gewald, Hinfelaar and Macola (eds.), *One Zambia*, pp. 17-44.

Makumbi, Jonas A. *Maliro Ndi Miyambo Ya Achewa*. Blantyre: Dzuka Publishing CompanyLtd, 1965

Mamdani, Mahmood. *Citizen and Subject: Contemporary Africa and the Legacy of Late Colonialism*. Princeton, NJ, Princeton University Press, 1996.

Marwick, M.G. "History and Tradition in East Central Africa through the Eyes of the Northern Rhodesia Chewa." *Journal of African History* 4, 3 (1963), pp. 375-390.

Matongo, Albert B.K. "Popular Culture in a Colonial Society: Another Look at Mbeni and Kalela Dance on the Copperbelt, 1930-1964," in Chipungu (ed.), *Guardians in their Time*, pp. 180-210.

McKittrick, Meredith. *To Dwell Secure: Generation, Christianity, and Colonialism in Ovamboland*. Portsmouth NH, Heinemann; Oxford: James Currey and Cape Town: David Philip, 2002.

Maxwell, David. *Christians and Chiefs: A Social History of the Hwesa People c. 1870-1990s*. Edinburgh: Edinburgh University Press, 1999.

_____. "The Spirit and the Scapular: Pentecostal and Catholic Interactions in Northern District, Zimbabwe, in the 1950s and 1960s." *Journal of Southern African Studies* 23, 2 (1997), pp. 283-300.

Meebelo, Henry. *Reaction to Colonialism: A Prelude to the Politics of Independence in Northern Zambia, 1893-1939*. Manchester: Manchester University Press, 1971.

Mitchell, Clyde J. "Kalela Dance: Aspects of Relationship among Urban African in Northern Rhodesia." *Rhodes-Livingstone Papers* 27. Manchester: Manchester University Press, 1956.

Molteno, Robert. "Cleavage and Conflict in Zambian Politics: A Study in Sectionalism," in William Tordoff (ed.), *Politics in Zambia*. Manchester: Manchester University Press. 1975, pp. 62-106.

Moomba, Jotham C. "Peasant Differentiation and Rural Party Politics in Colonial Zambia," *Journal of Southern African Studies* 11, 2 (1985), pp. 281-294.

Mulenga, Friday E. "Fighting for democracy of the pocket: The labour movement of the Third Republic." in Gewald, Hinfelaar and Macola (eds.), *One Zambia, Many Histories*, pp. 243-258.

117

Bibliography

Mulford, David. *The Northern Rhodesia General Election, 1962*. London: Oxford University Press, 1964.

_____. *Northern Rhodesia Constitution*. Nairobi: Oxford University press. 1964.

_____. *Zambia: The Politics of Independence, 1957-1964*. London: Oxford University Press, 1967.

Msiko, A.K. and Elizabeth Mumba. "A History of Adult Education in Zambia," in H.J. Msango, E.C. Mumba and A.L. Sikwebele (eds.). *Selected Topics in Philosophy and Education*. Lusaka: The University of Zambia Press, 2000.

Mwale, E.B. *Za Achewa*. Lusaka: Macmillan, 1982.

Mwanakatwe, John. *The Growth of Education in Zambia since Independence*. Lusaka: Oxford University Press, 1974.

Mwangilwa, Goodwin. *Harry Nkumbula: A Biography*. Lusaka: Multimedia Publications, 1982.

Phiri, Bizeck Jube. *A Political History of Zambia: From the Colonial Period to the 3rd Republic*. Trenton, NJ and Asamara: Africa World Press, 2004.

Pritchett, James Anthony. *Lunda-Ndembu: Style, Change and Social Transformation in South Central Africa*. Madison: University of Wisconsin Press, 2001.

_____. *Friends for Life, Friends for Death: Cohorts and Consciousness among the Lunda-Ndembu*. Charlottesville and London: Virginia University Press, 2007.

Ranger, T.O. *Revolt in Southern Rhodesia, 1896-7*. London: Heinemann, 1967.

_____. "The Mwana Lesa Movement of 1925," in T. Ranger and J. Weller (eds.), *Themes in the Christian History of Central Africa*. Berkeley and Los Angeles: University of California Press, 1975.

Rasmussen, Thomas. "The Popular basis of anti-colonial protest," in William Tordoff (ed.), *Politics in Zambia*. Manchester: Manchester University Press, 1975.

Schoffellers, Matthew. "The Resistance of Nyau Societies to the Roman Catholic Mission in Colonial Malawi," in T.O. Ranger and I.N. Kimambo (eds.), *The Historical Study of African Religion with Special Reference to East and Central Africa*. Nairobi: Heinemann, 1972, pp. 252-271.

Sklar, Richard L. "Zambia's Response to the Rhodesian Unilateral Declaration of Independence," in Tordoff (ed.), *Politics in Zambia*, pp. 320-362.

Snelson, Peter. *Education and Development in Northern Rhodesia, 1883-1945*. Lusaka: Neczam, 1974.

Turner, Victor. *Schism and Continuity in an African Society: A Study of Ndembu Village Life*. Manchester: Manchester University Press, 1957.

_____. *The Drum of Affliction: A Study of the Religious Processes among the Ndembu of Zambia*. Oxford: Oxford University Press, 1969.

_____. *The Forest of Symbols: Aspects of Ndembu Ritual*. Ithaca, NY.: Cornell University Press, 1967.

_____. *Revelation and Divination in Ndembu Ritual*. Ithaca, NY and London: Cornell University Press, 1975.

Vine, Alex. *RENAMO: Terrorism in Mozambique*. University of York; Centre of African Studies; London: James Currey; Bloomington and Indianapolis, 1991.

Von Donge, Jan Kees. "Zambia, Kaunda and Chiluba: Enduring Patterns of Political Culture," in John A. Wiseman (ed.). *Democracy and Political Change in Sub-Saharan Africa* (London: NewYork: Routledge, 1995.

Wina, Sikota. *Night Without a President*. Lusaka: Multimedia, 1985.

Zeleza, Tiyambe. "The Political Economy of British Colonial Development and Welfare in British Africa." *TransAfrican Journal of History* 15 (1985), pp. 139-161.

Zulu, Alexander Grey. *Memoirs of Alexander Grey Zulu*. Ndola: Printpak, 2007.

(ii) Dissertation, Speeches and other sources

Chabatama, Mebbiens Chewe. "Peasant Farming: The State and Food Security in North-Western Province of Zambia, 1902-1964." PhD dissertation: University of Toronto, 1992.

Datta, Kusum. "The Policy of Indirect Rule in Zambia (Northern Rhodesia), 1924-1953." PhD dissertation: London University, 1976.

Gawa Undi X, "Speech during the Golden Jubilee Cerebrations." Mkaika Traditional Headquarters, Katete, on 3 March 2003."

Kakoma, Ben C. "Colonial Administration in Northern Rhodesia: A Case Study of Administration in Mwinilunga District, 1900-1939." M.A. dissertation: University of Auckland, 1971.

Kalusa, Walima T. "Disease and the Remaking of Missionary Medicine in North-   Western Zambia: A Case of Mwinilunga District, 1902-1964." PhD dissertation: Johns Hopkins University, 2003.

Langworthy III, Harry Wells. "A History of Undi's Kingdom to 1890: Aspects of Chewa History in East Central Africa." PhD dissertation: Boston University, 1969.

Livingstone, David and Charles. *Narrative of the Expedition to the Zambezi and its Tributaries*. New York: Harper and Brother, 1866.

Lungu, Andrew. "Harmony Provided Through Kulamba Traditional Ceremony." http://www.times.co.zm/

Mtonga, Mapopa. "The Drama of Gule Wamkulu: A Study of the Nyau as Practised by the Chewa of Eastern Province of Zambia," MA dissertation: University of Ghana, Institute of African Studies, Legon, 1980.

Mtshali, Benedict V. "Zambia's Foreign Policy: The Dilemma of a New State." PhD dissertation: NewYork University, 1972.

Mukelebai Songiso, "Zambia's Role in Southern Africa." MA dissertation: University of Zambia, 1989.

Mulenga, Nebert. "Discerning the Different Faces of Kulamba Kubwalo." http://www.times.co.zm/news/

Mwanawasa, Levy Patrick. "Speech by His Excellency the President of the Republic of Zambia, SC, on the Occasion of the 2007 Kulamba Traditional Ceremony of the Chewa People of Malawi, Mozambique, and Zambia on the 25th August, 2007 at Mkaika Palace in Katete."

Bibliography

Pritchett, James Anthony, "The Kanongesha Lunda of Mwinilunga, Zambia," PhD dissertation: Harvard University, 1989.

Silva, Sonia. "Vicarious Selves: Divination Baskets and Angolan Refugees in Zambia," PhD dissertation: Indiana University, 1999.

Zimba, Enestle. "Discover Kulamba: A Three-Nation Traditional Ceremony." http://www.zambia-theAfrican-safari.com/Africa.

List of Informants

The occupations of the interviewees, places and dates of interviews are indicated in the text.

Banda, Alifasi Kafumu
Banda, Ferdinand M.
Banda Yasintha
Banda, Yohanne
Chigaga, Lyson Phiri
Chigwala, G.
Chikuta, Joseph Galeta
Chimbelekero, Kafuwa Yobe
Daka, Handsen
Daka, Lameck
Kasumba, Hilario
Moyo, Mailes
Mwale, Anelo Makowa
Phiri, Chafunya Alick
Phiri, Peter Chaima
Phiri, Kamlendo
Phiri, Kaseke
Phiri, Levison
Mama Nyangu
Nyirongo, Edward
Sakala, Teddy Abraham

120

INDEX

Index

Index

www.ingramcontent.com/pod-product-compliance
Lightning Source LLC
Chambersburg PA
CBHW011821280326
41932CB00021BA/3359

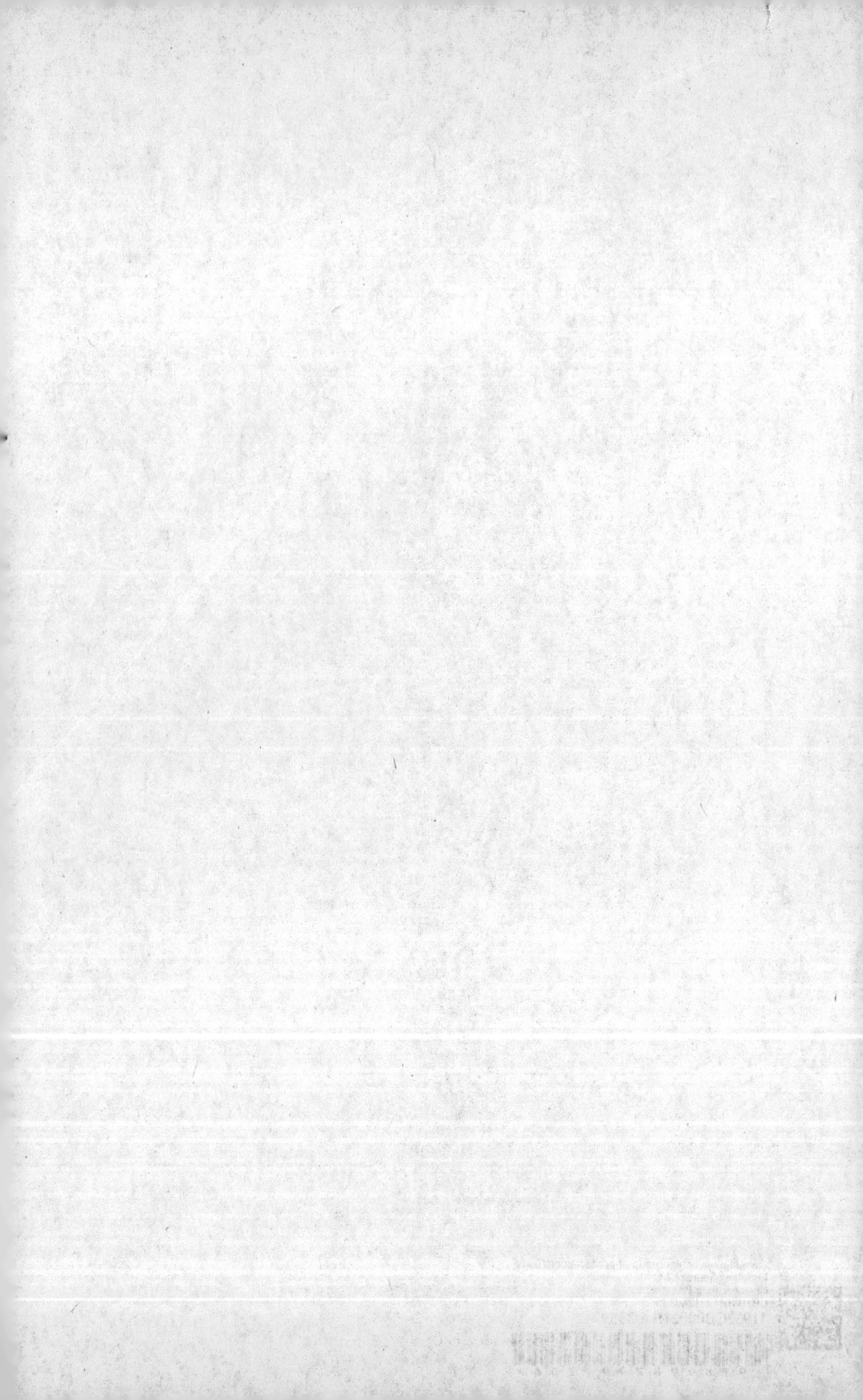